I0465610

Relaxing Dot To Dot For Adults
Extreme Stress Relieving Easy to Read Puzzles
From 150 to 650 Dots

By Laura's Dot to Dot Therapy

How To Use This Book

Hi! We're so glad you're a lover of puzzles and dot connecting- we are too!

Connecting the dots in this book is simple- just relax and follow the numbers in consecutive order, drawing a straight line between each one. Dot 1 will connect to dot 2 and so on and so forth until there are no more dots to connect. There's always another dot and you'll always find it. Connect every dot to discover the beautiful images they create.

In case you get lost or can't find a dot, never stress- there's an answer key at the back of the book that will show you exactly where each dot connects to the next. If you want to color your images, we encourage you to do so! Feel free to try all different colors and coloring mediums for your images!

If you find any errors or omissions in this book, email us at Laurasdottodot@gmail.com and please let us know! We want you to have the best dot to dot experience!

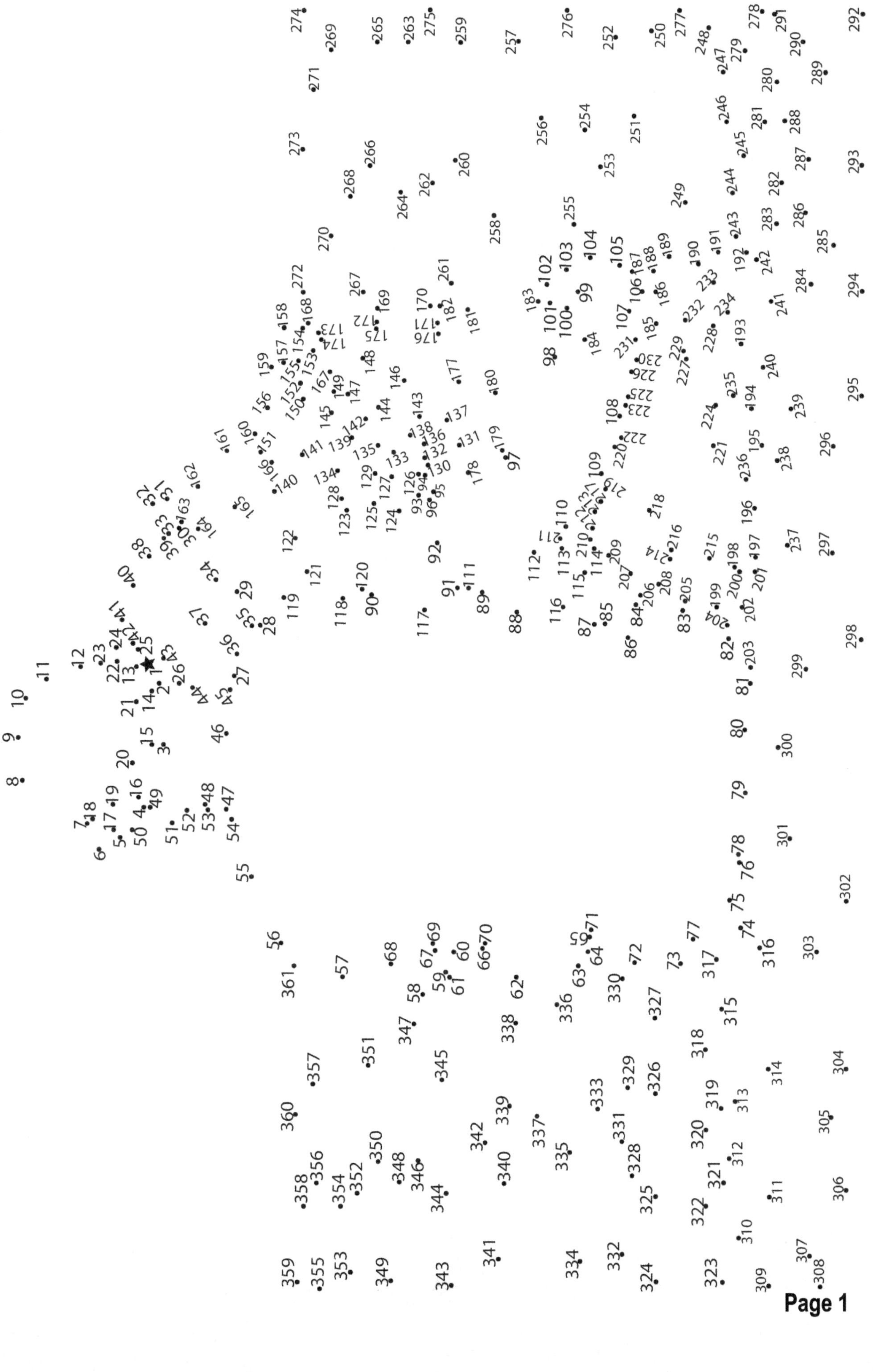

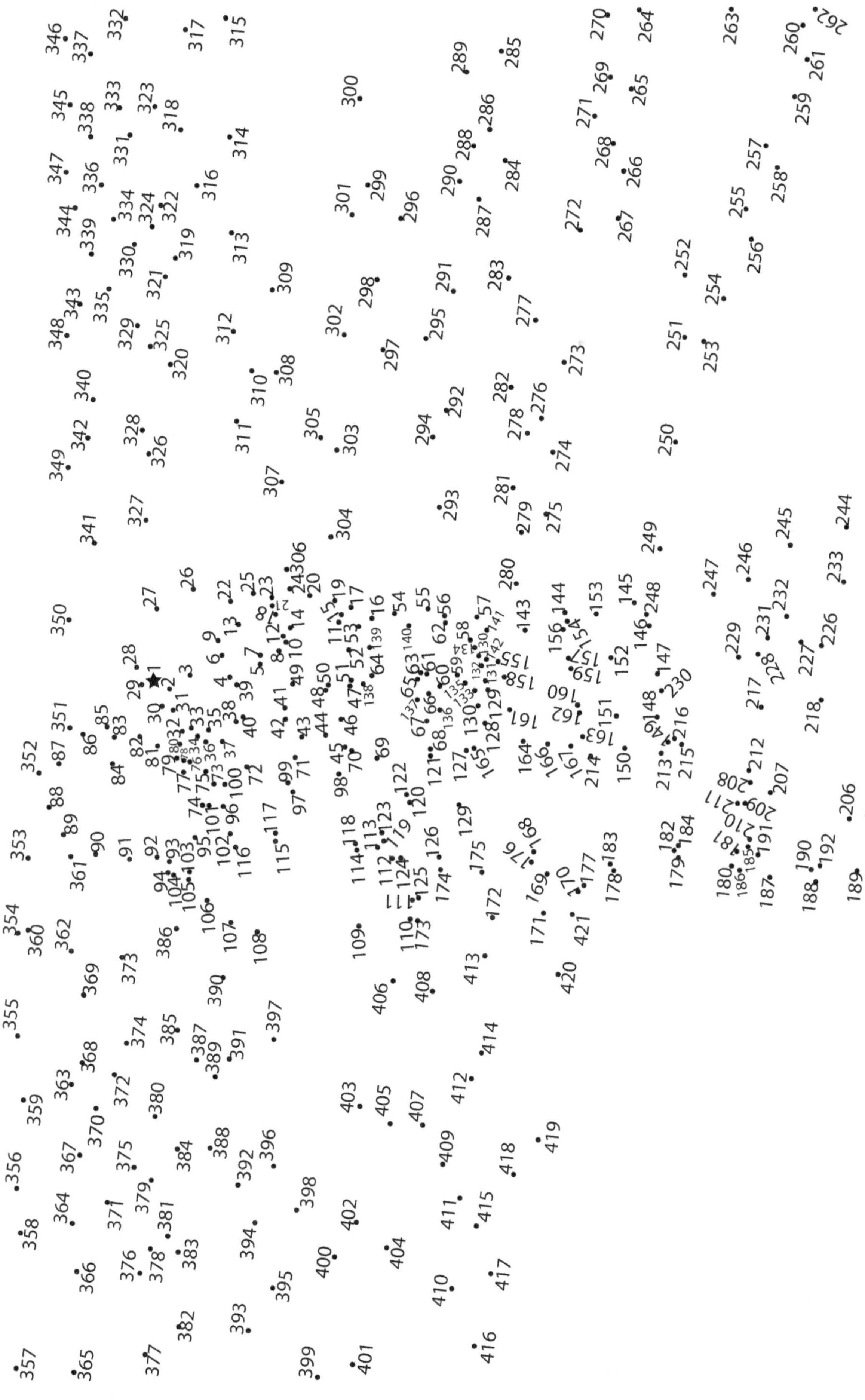

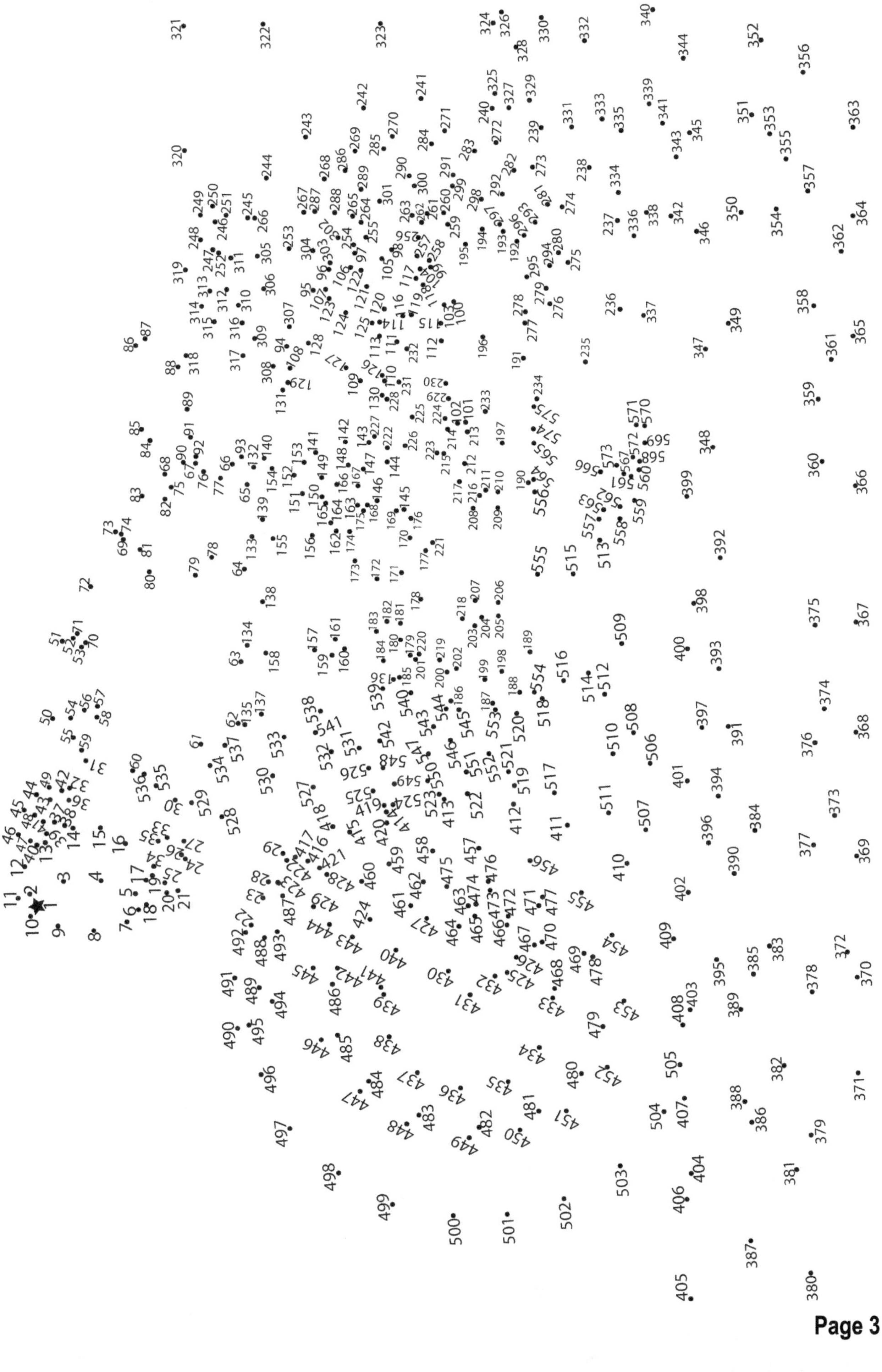

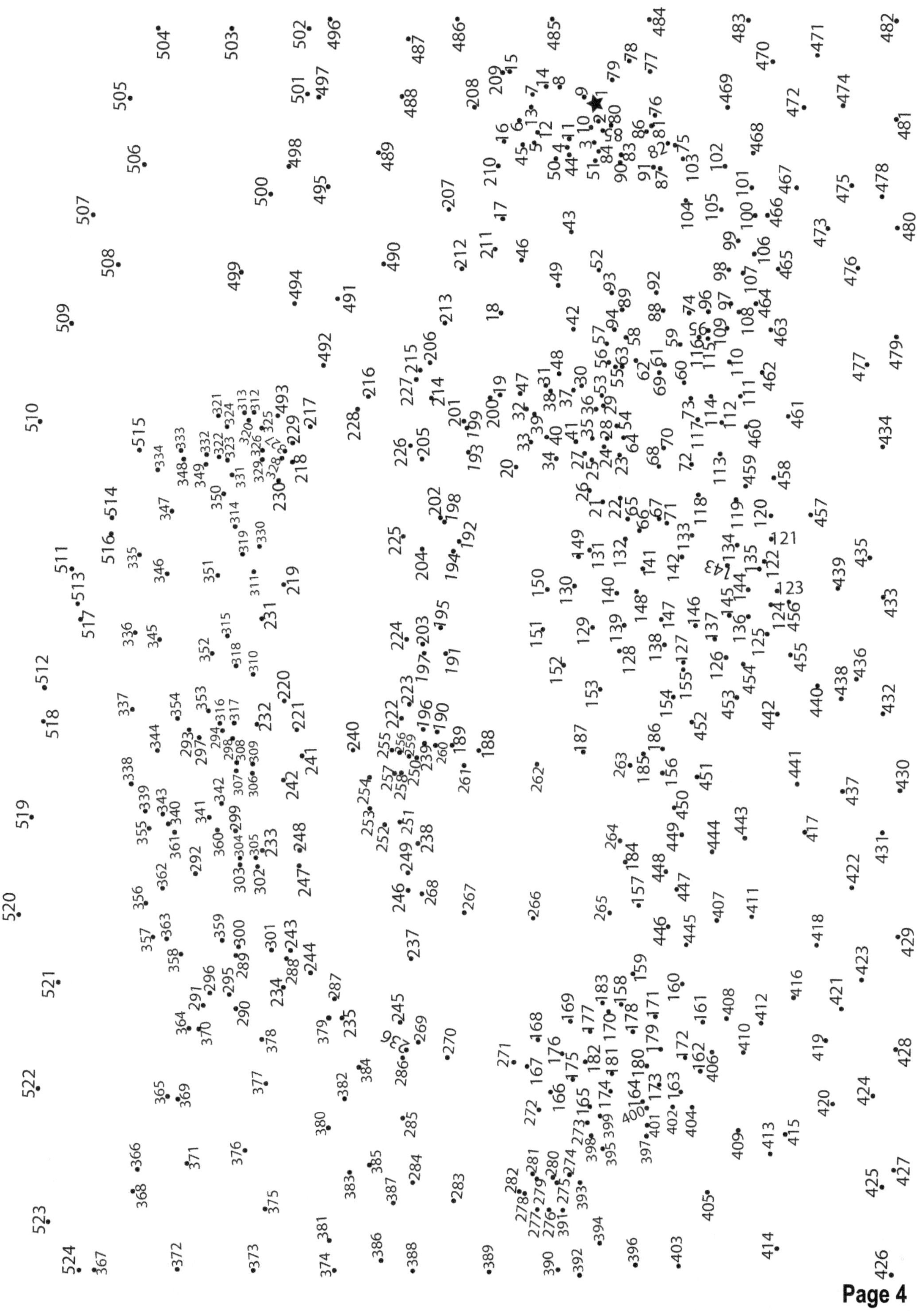

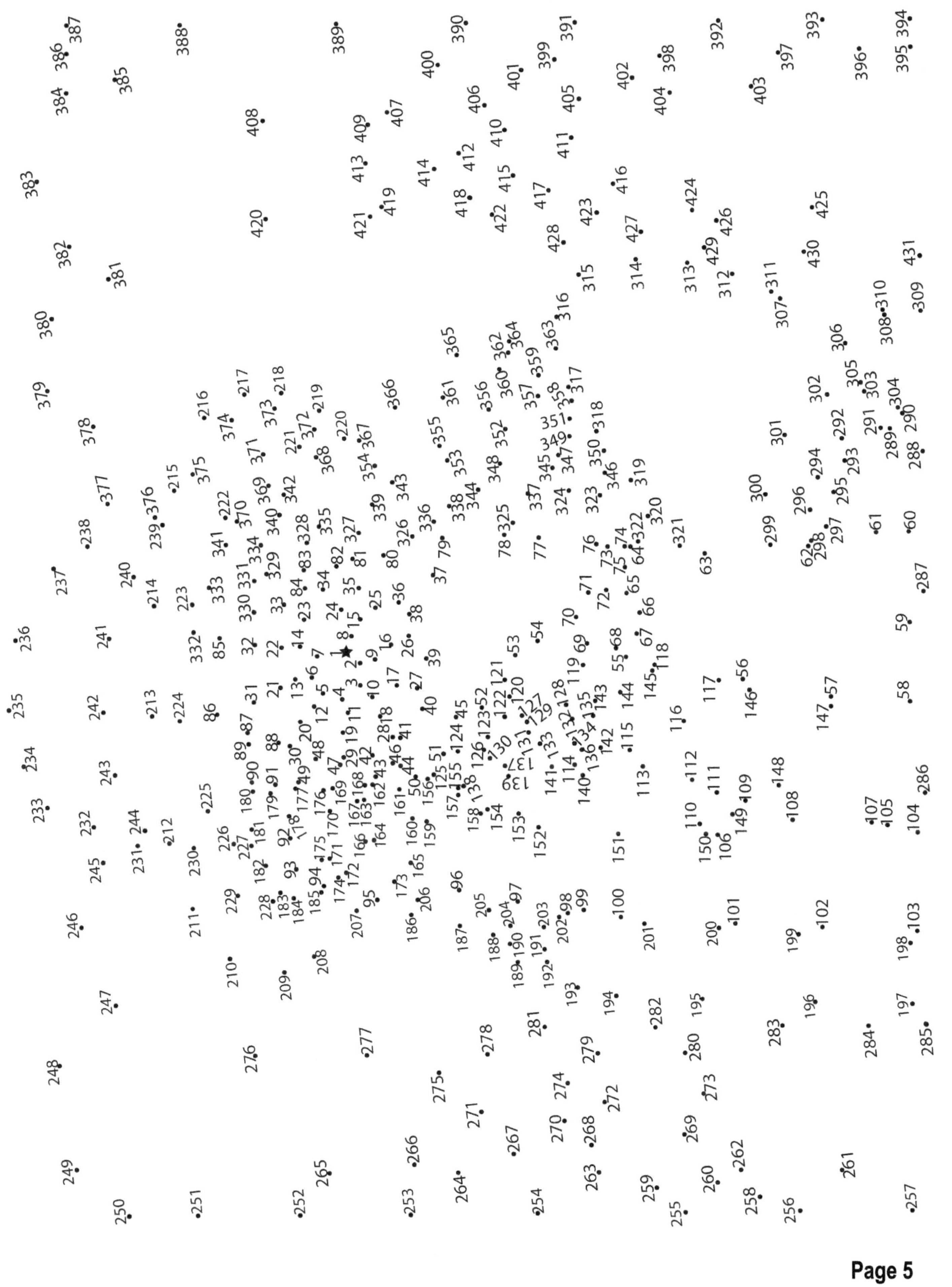

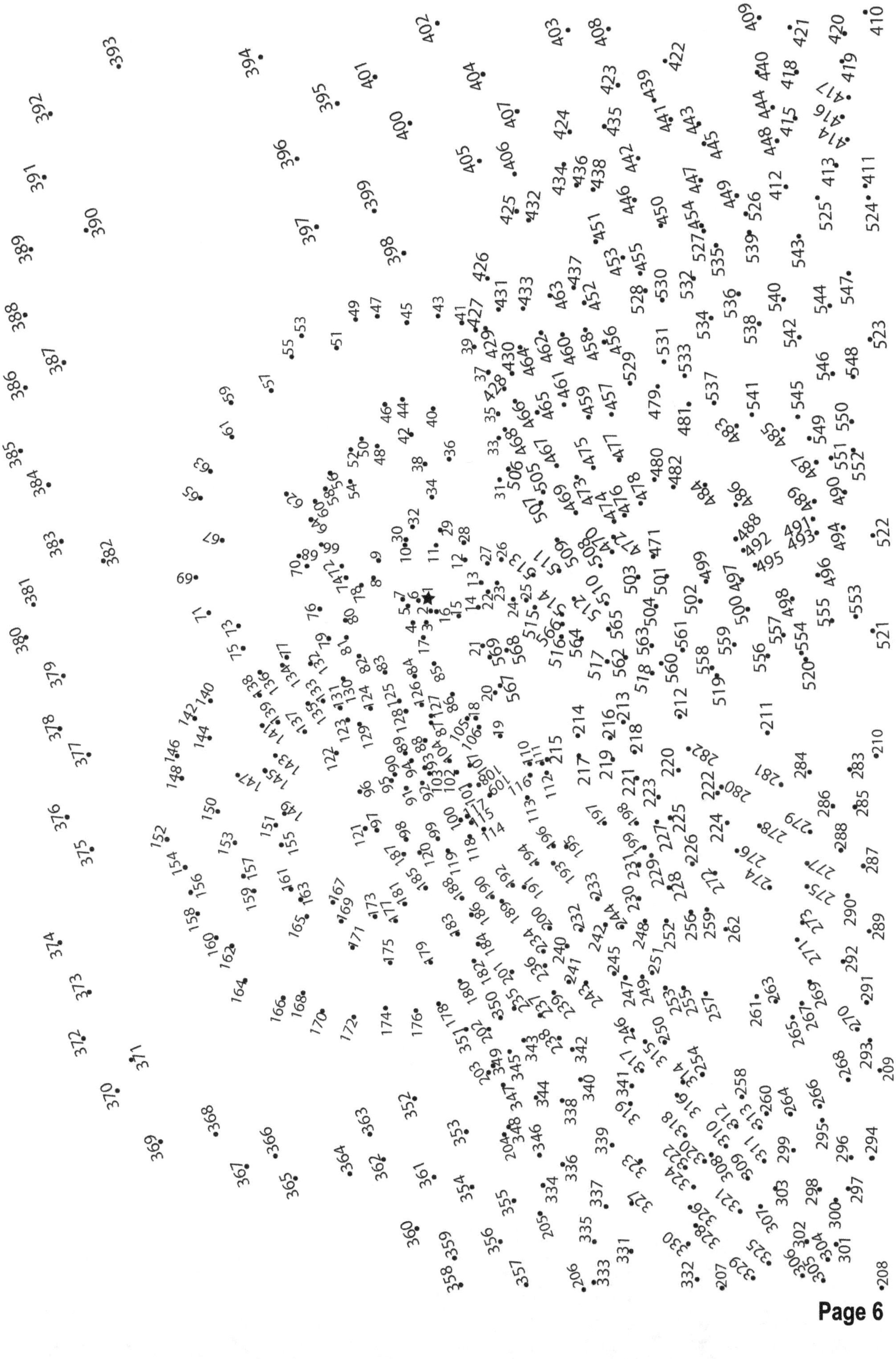

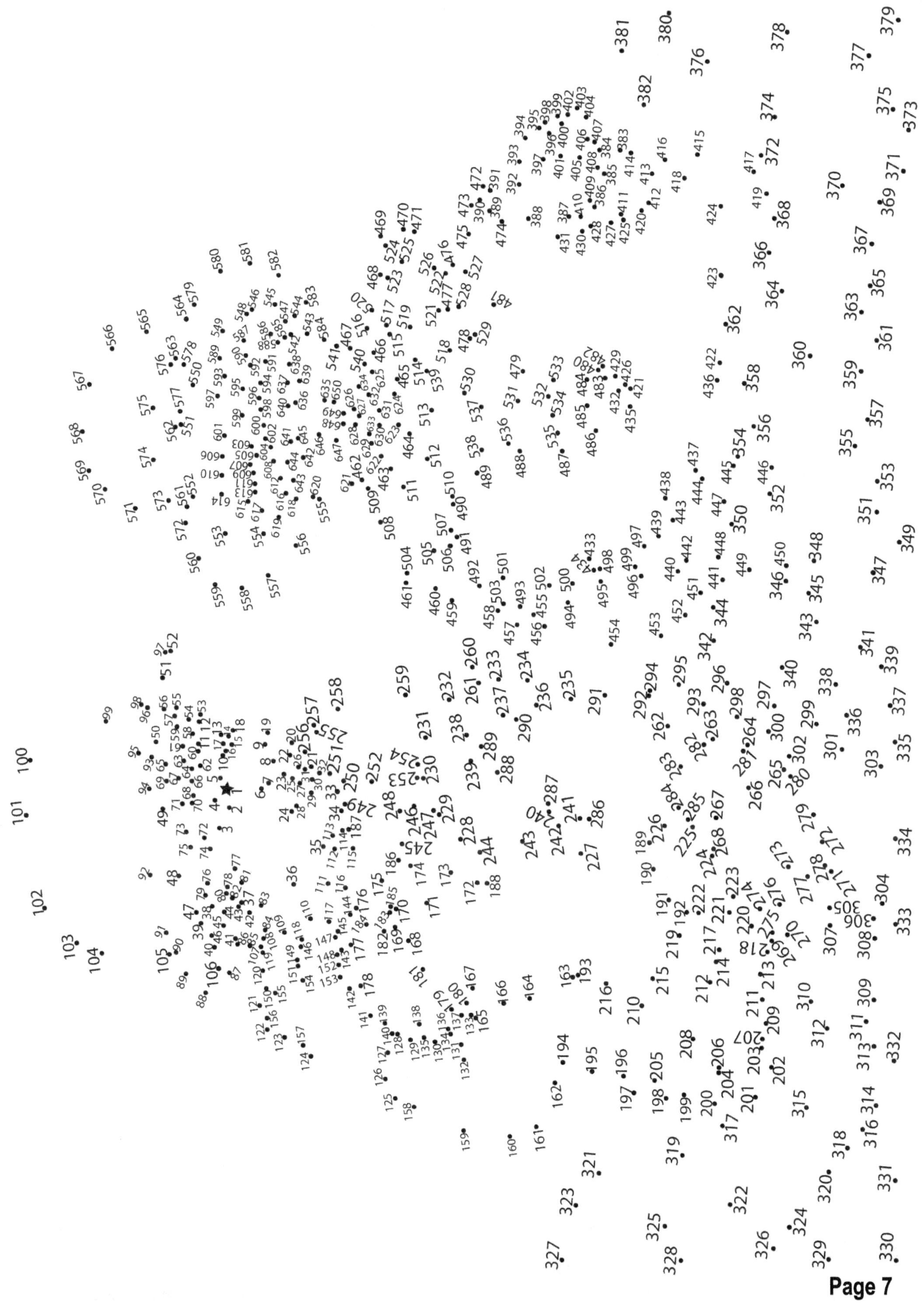

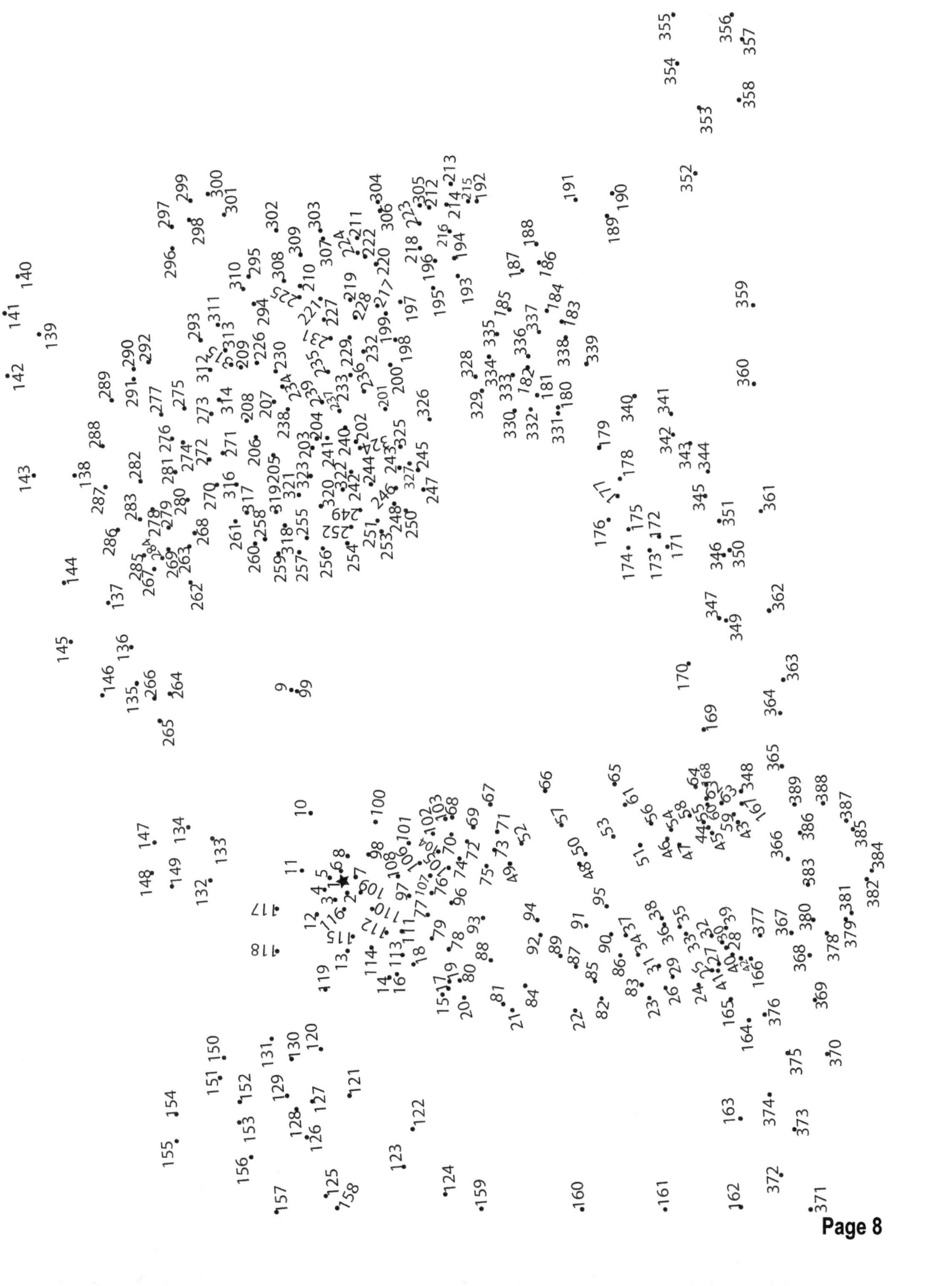

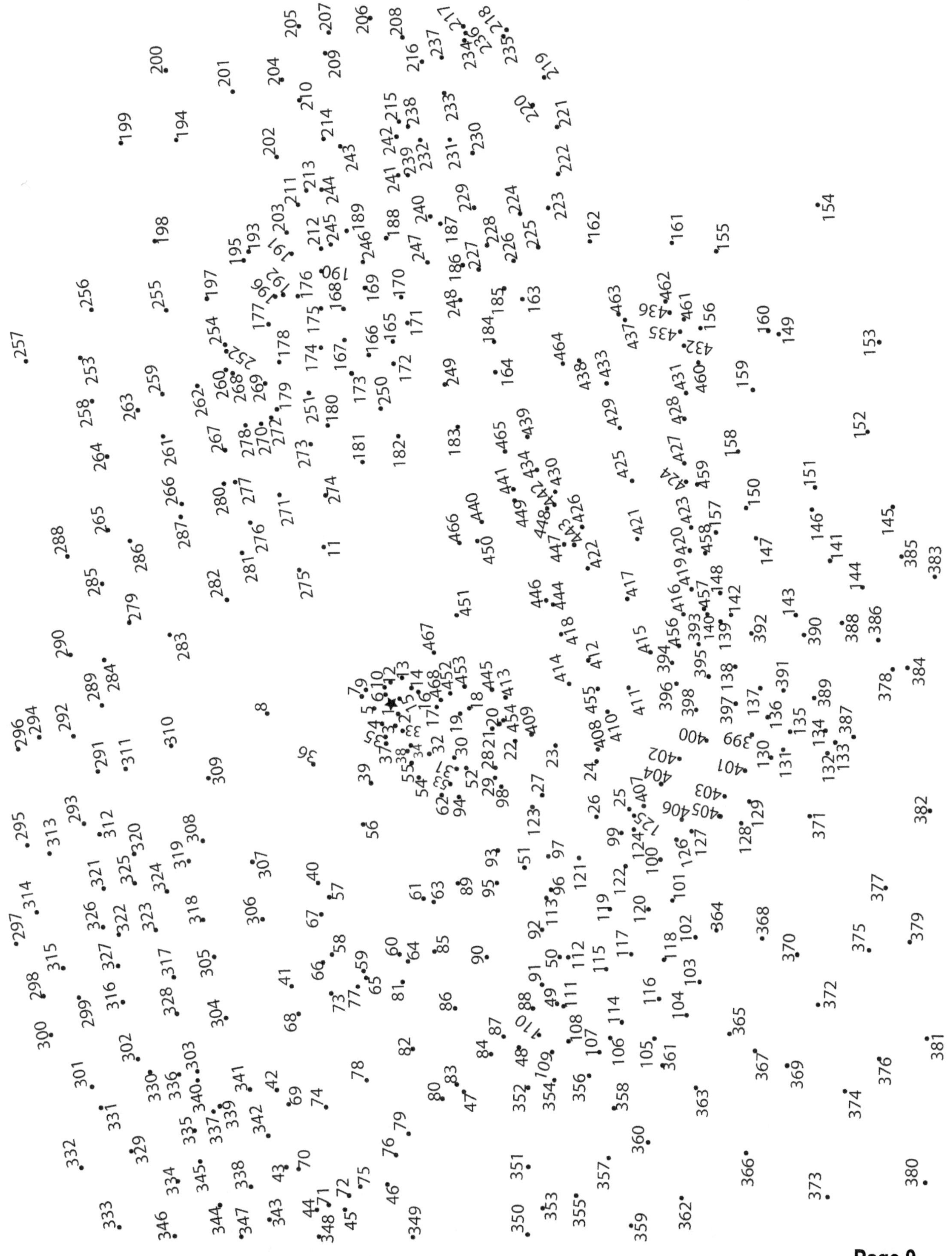

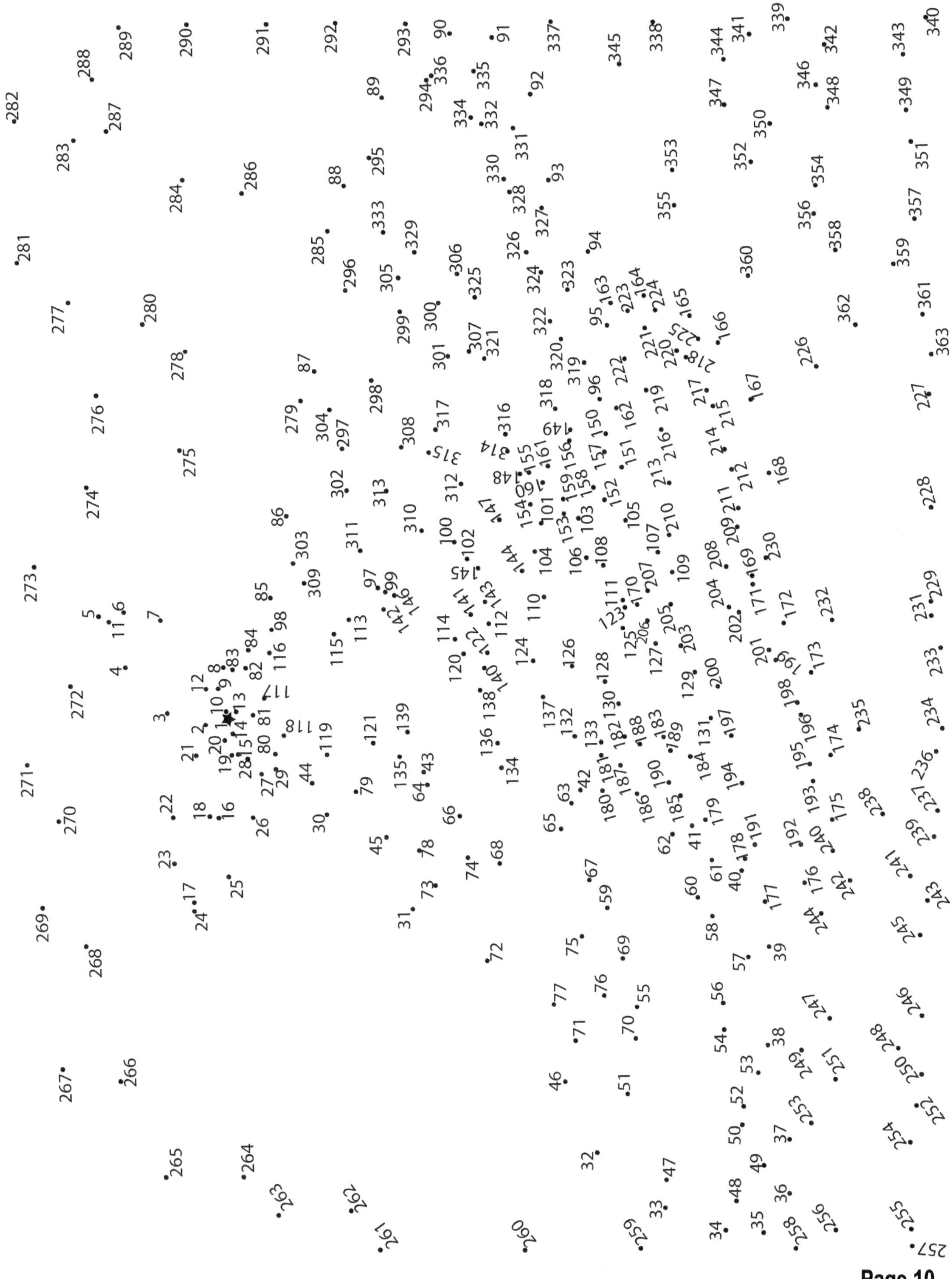

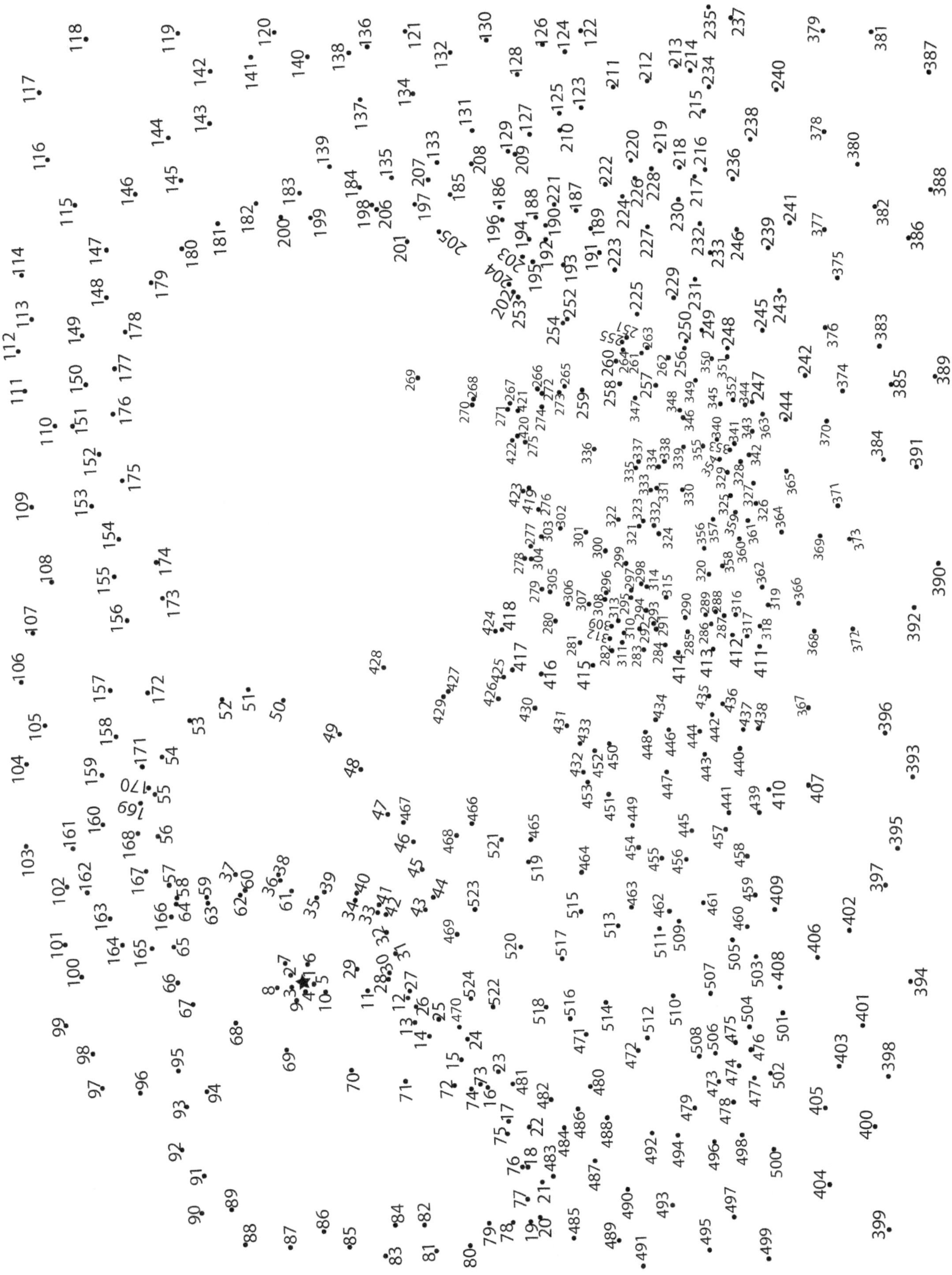

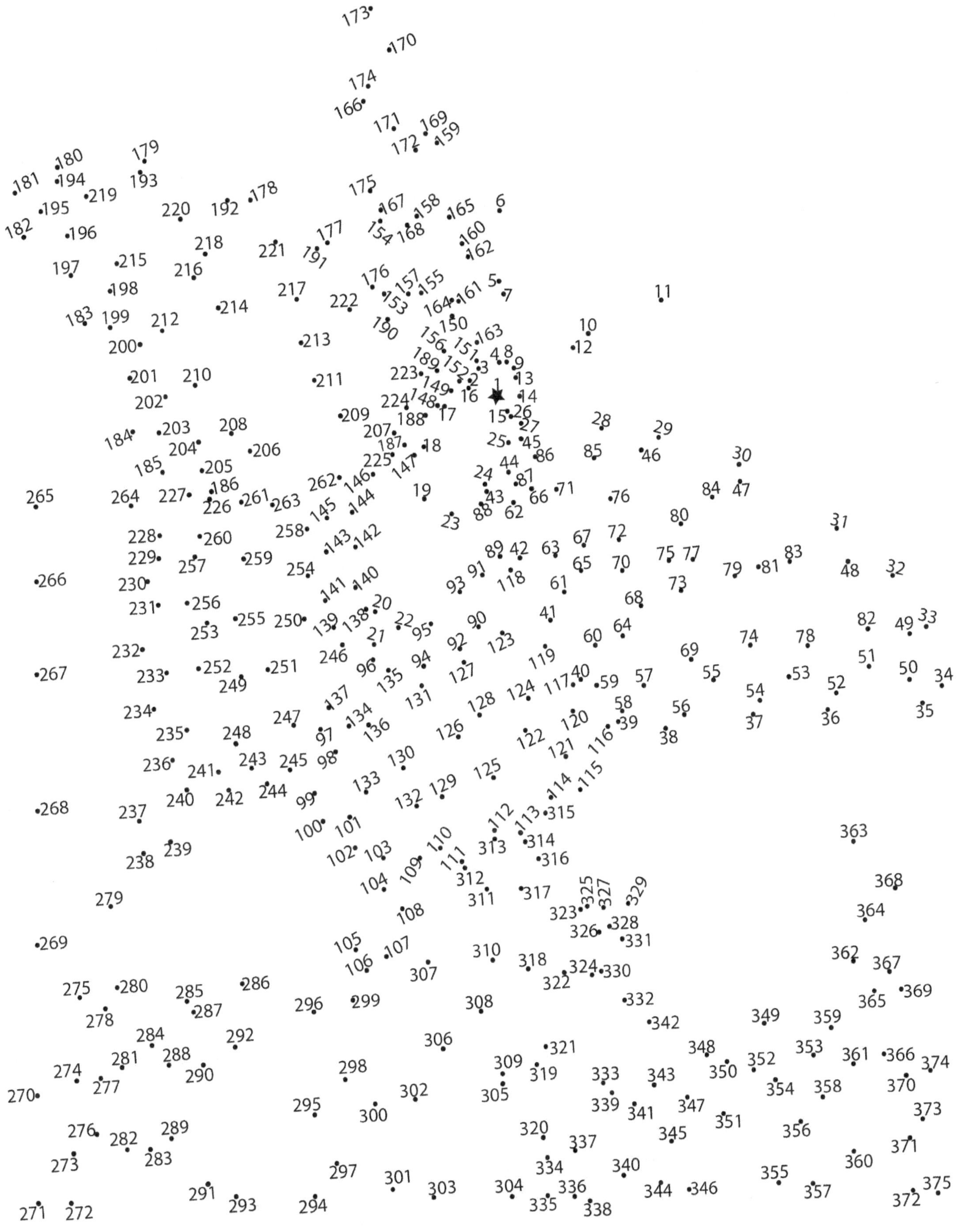

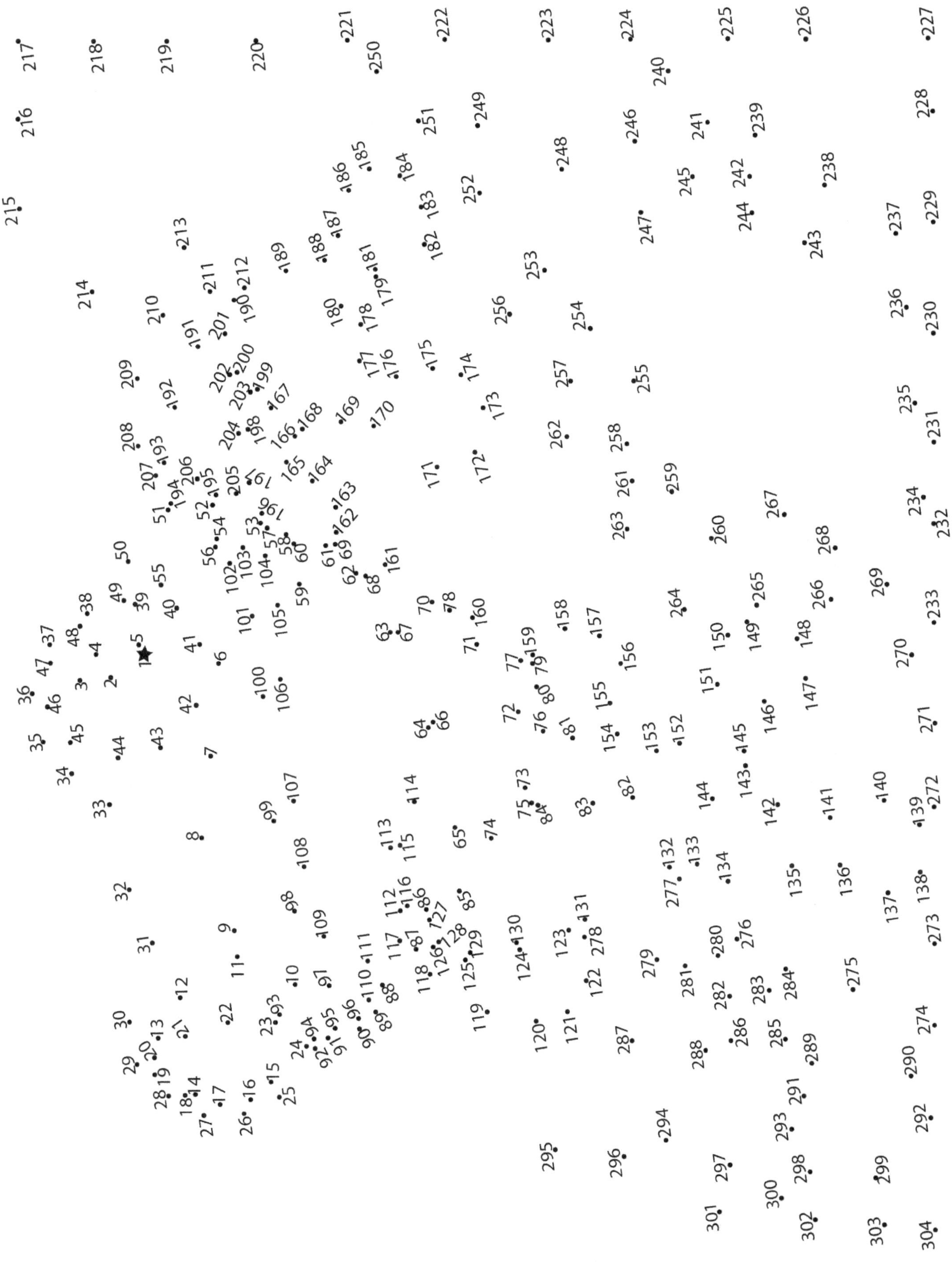

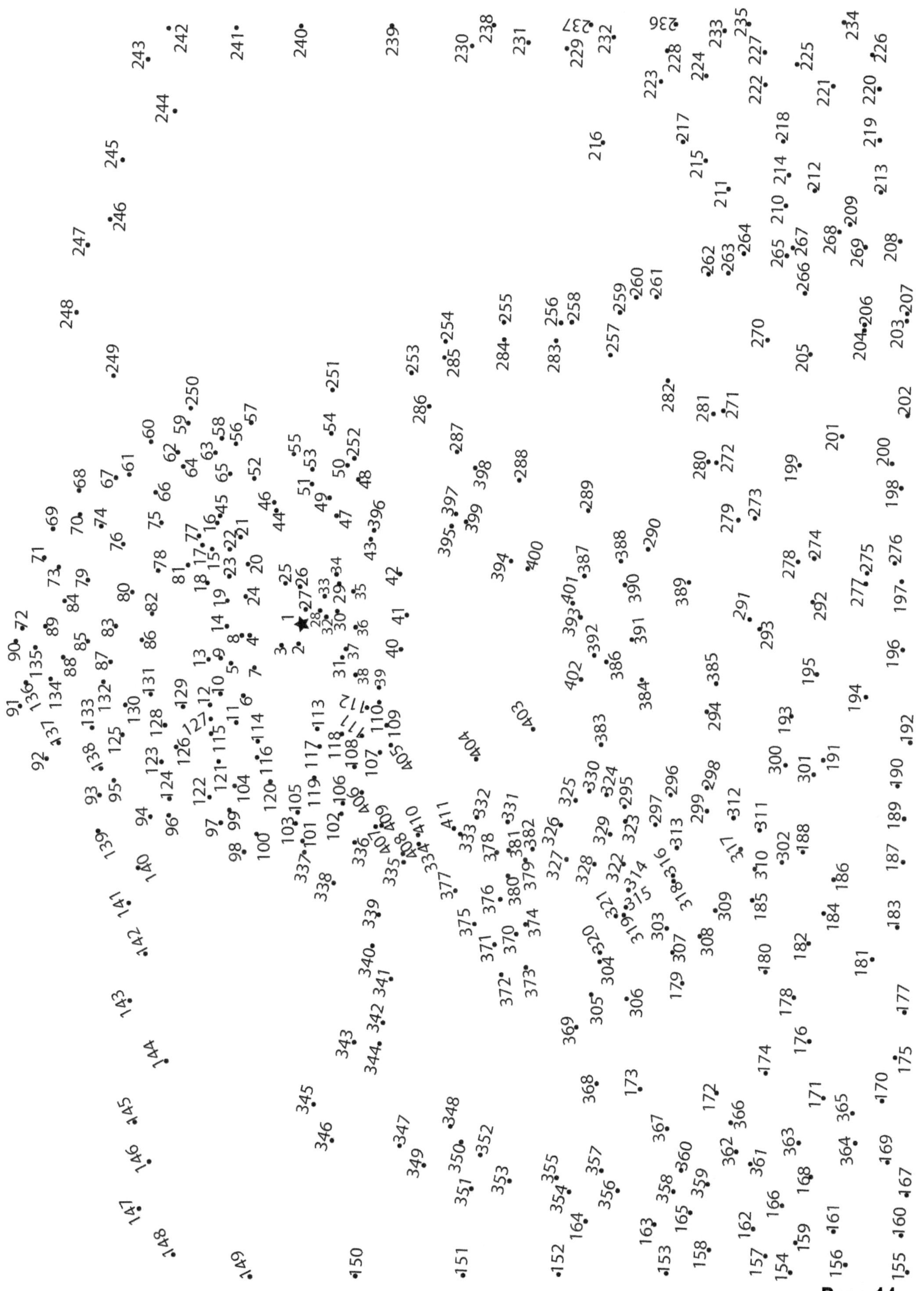

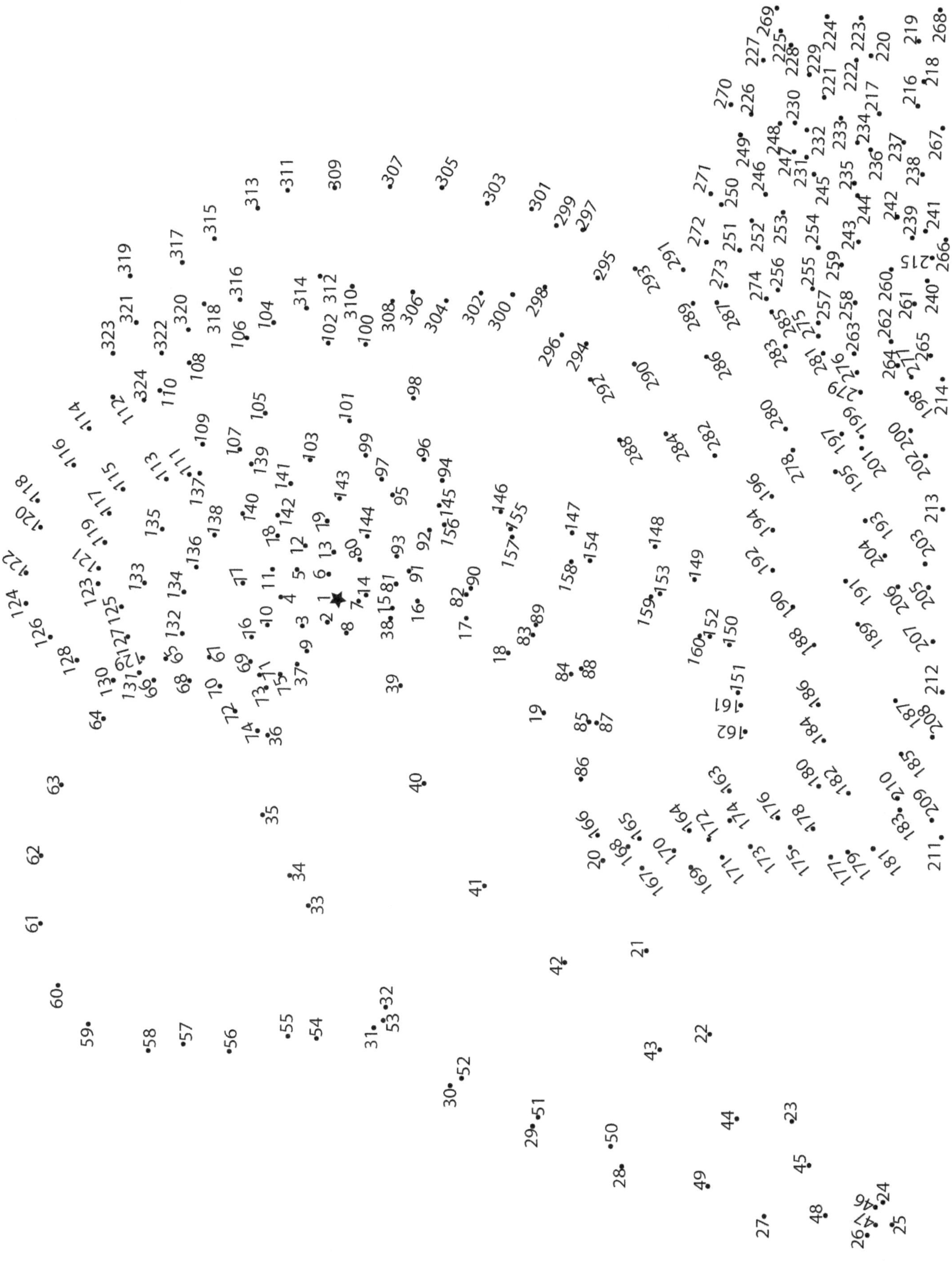

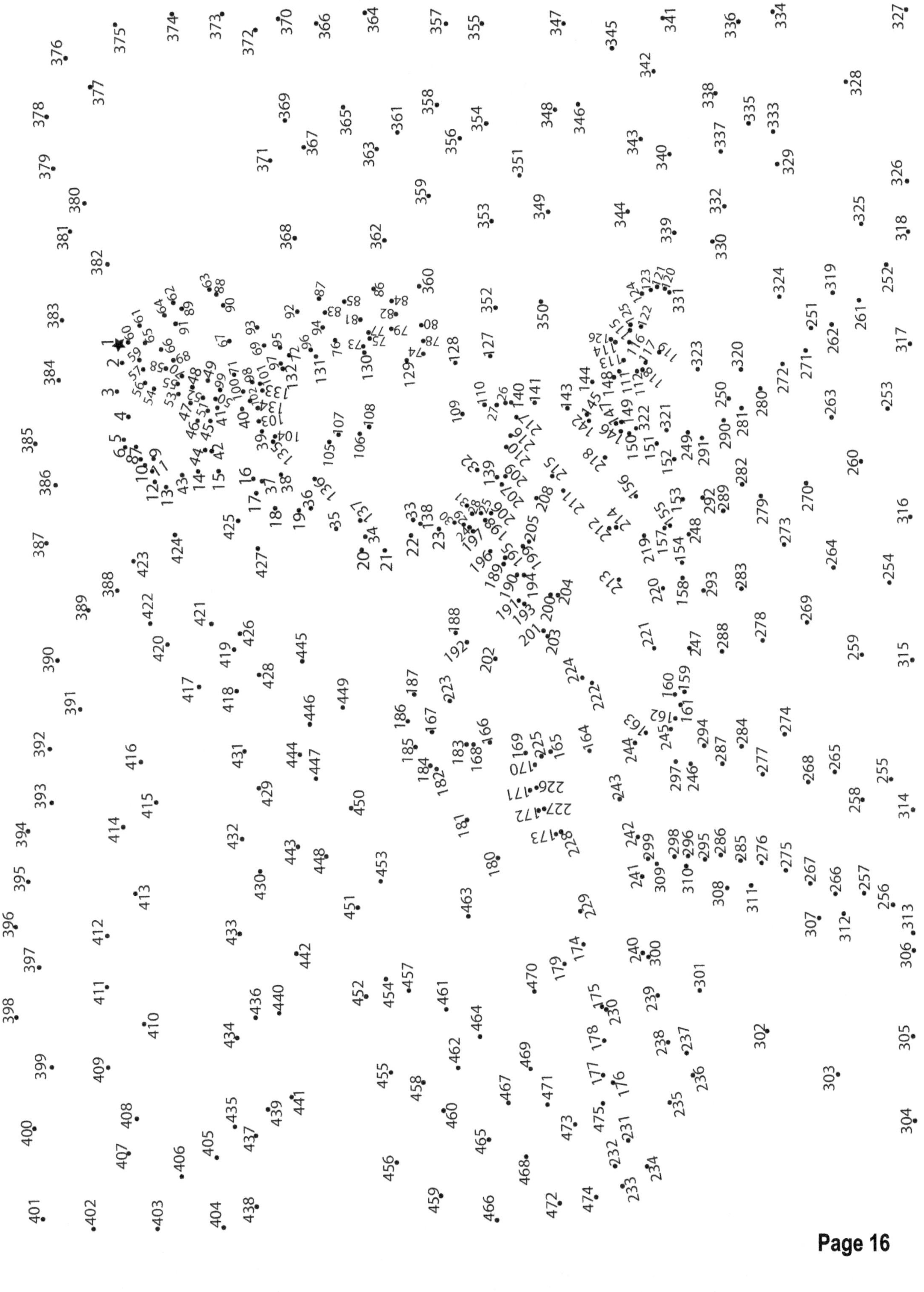

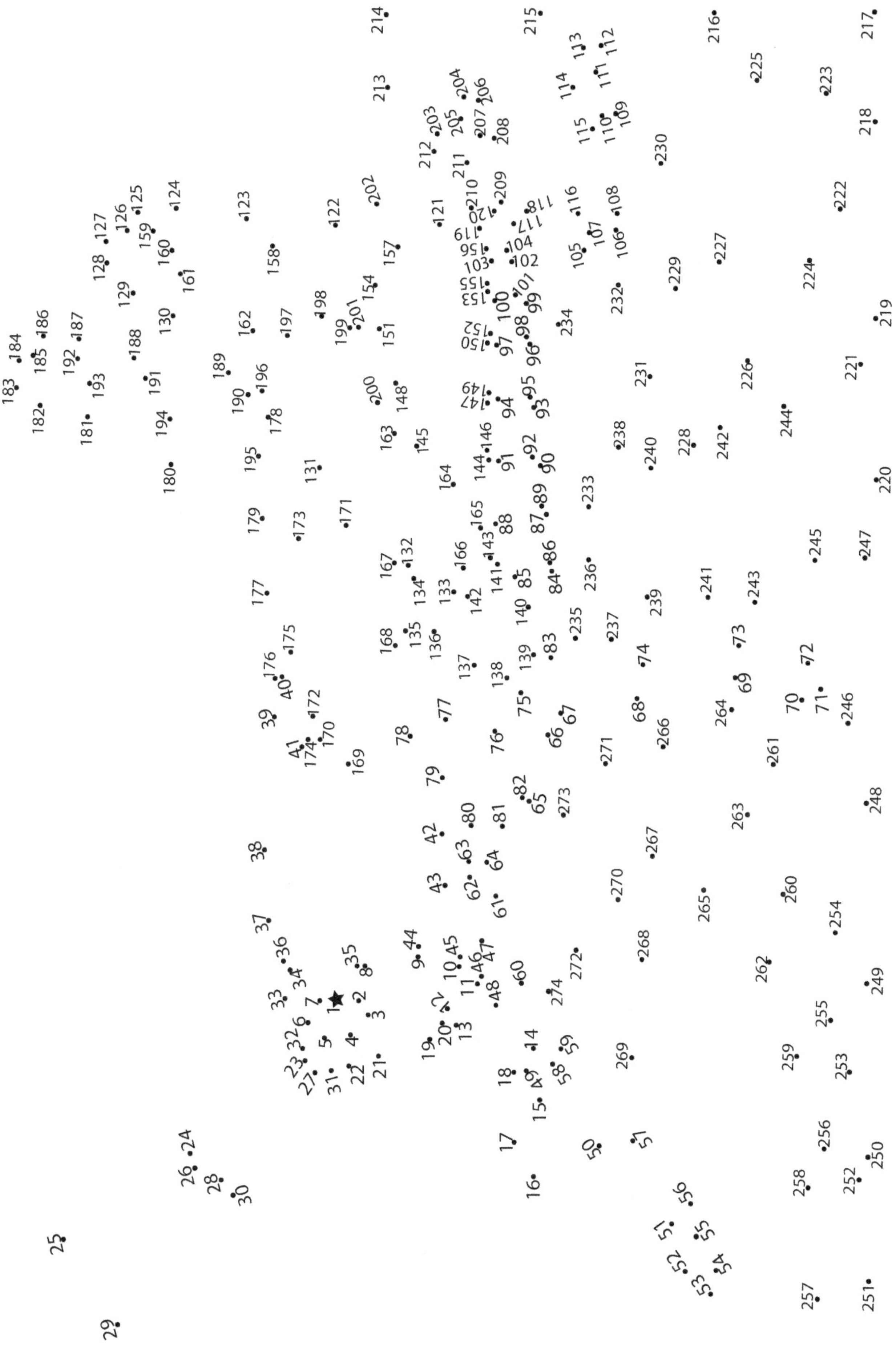

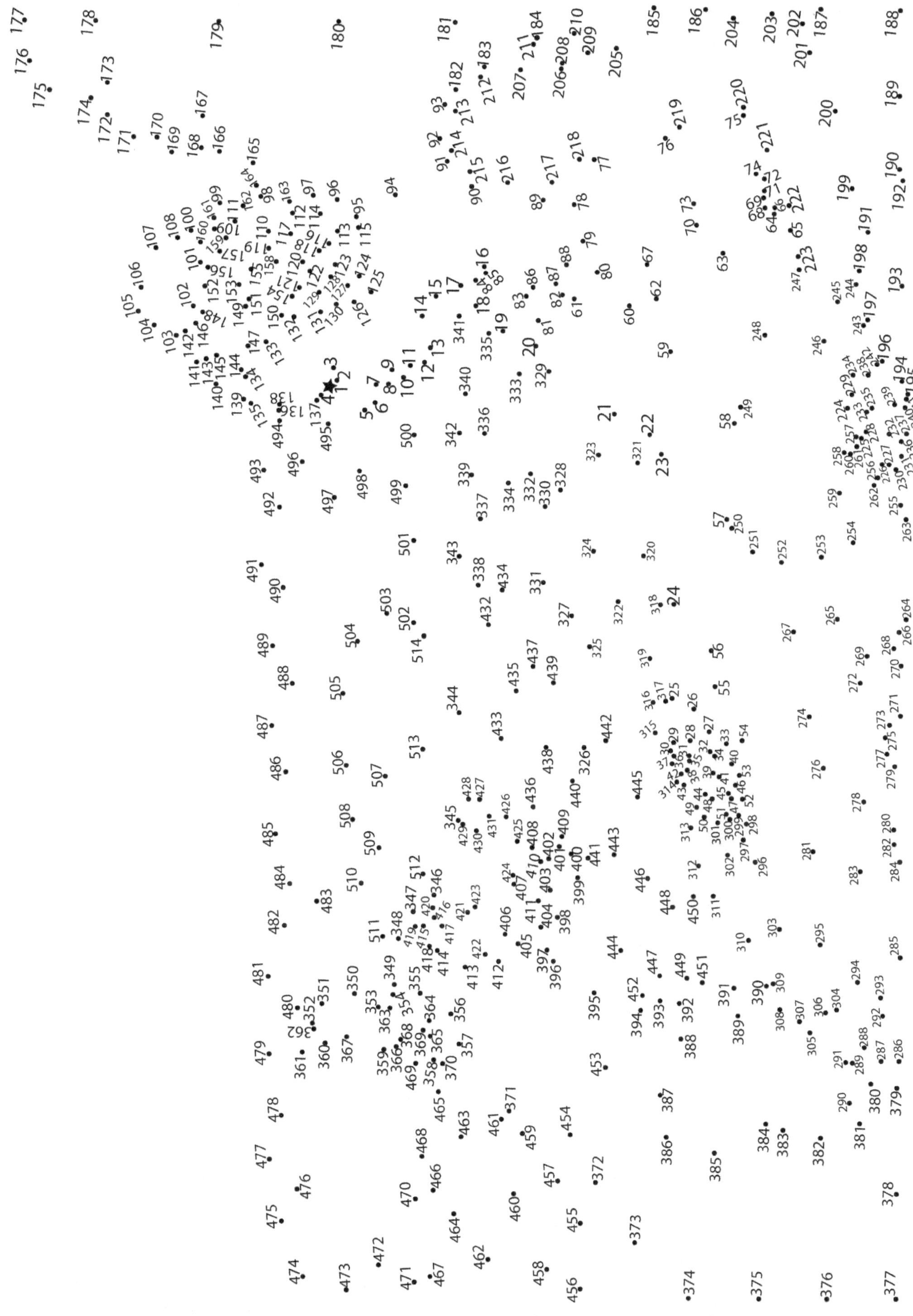

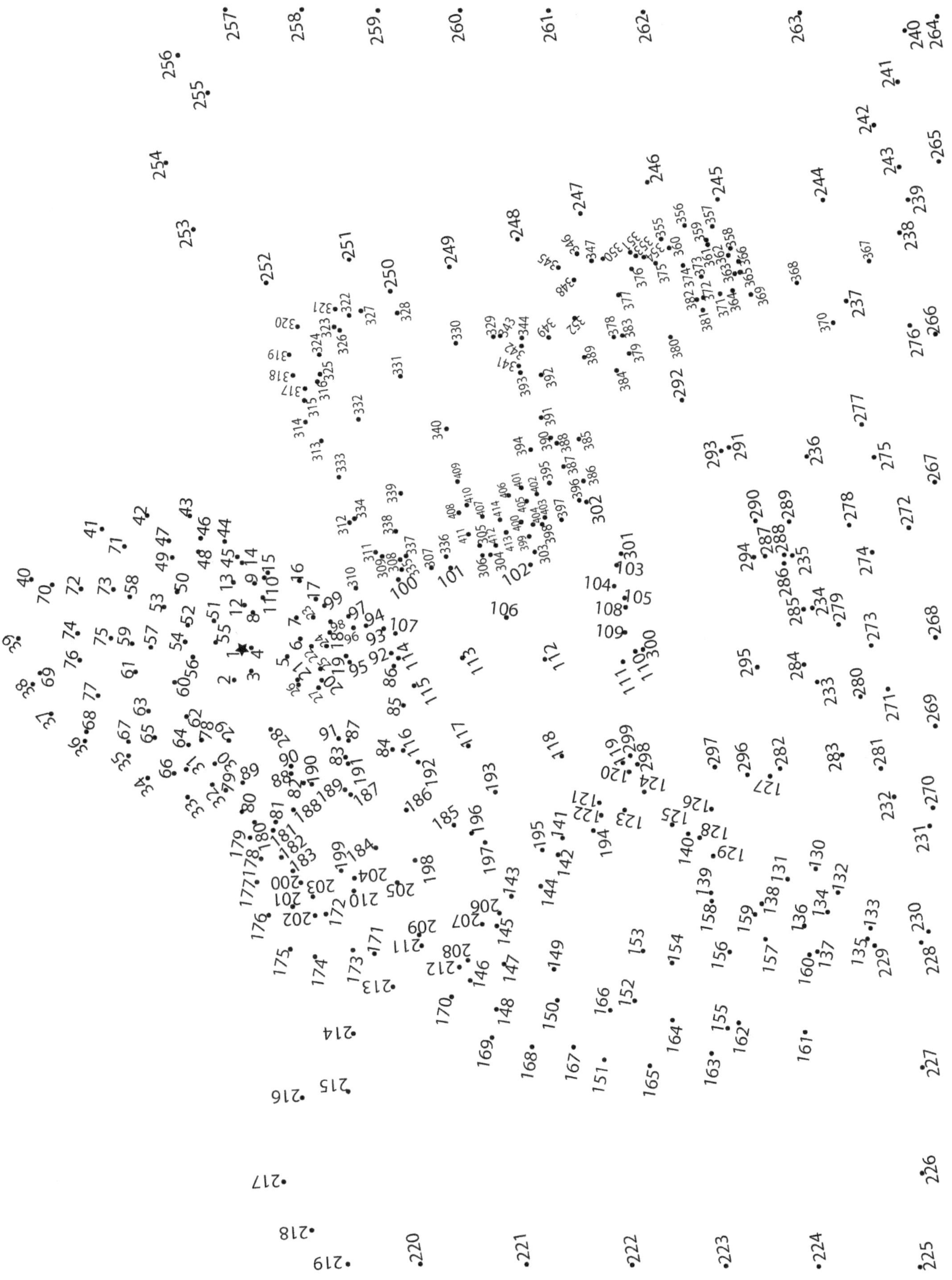

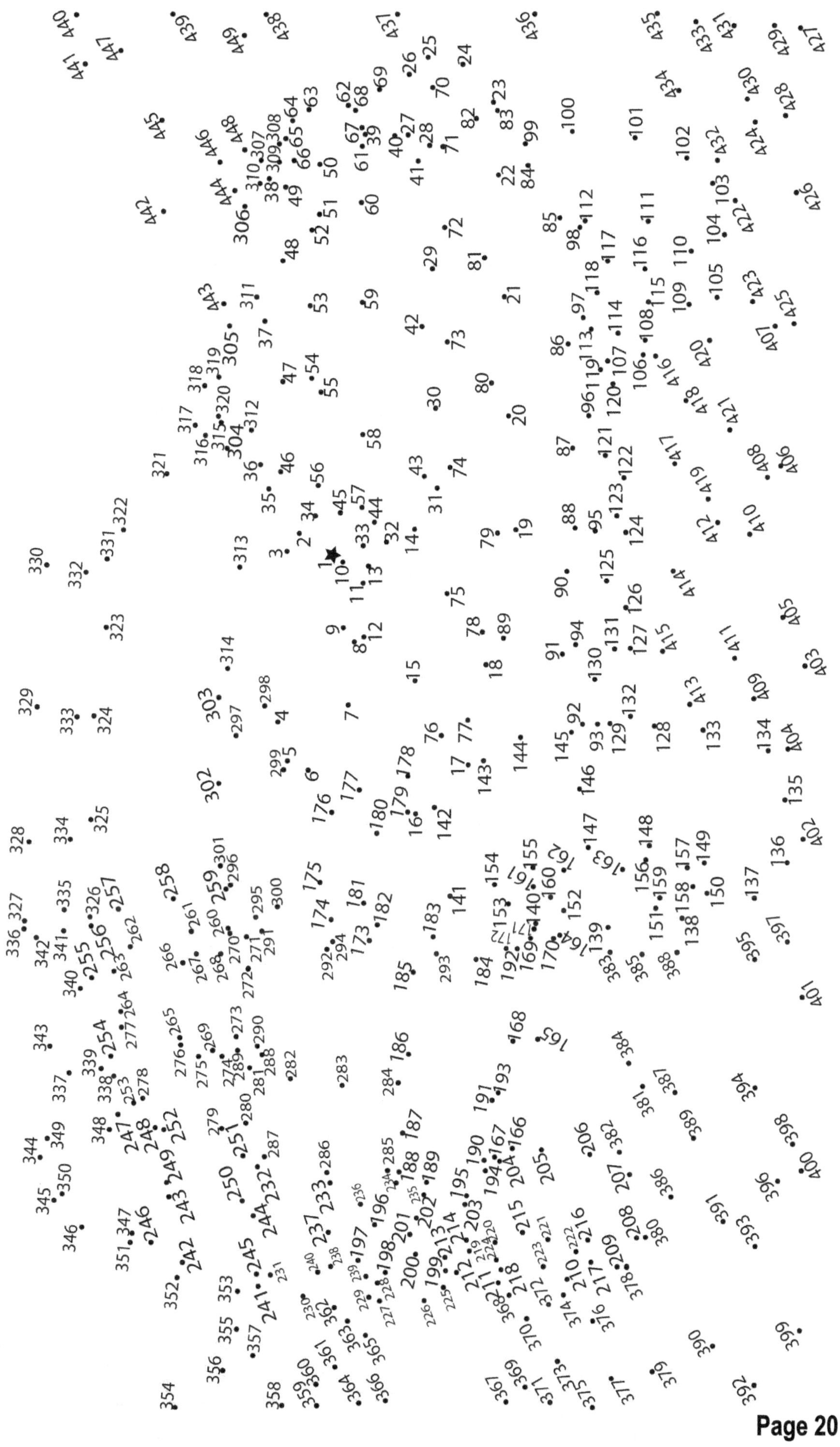

Enjoy bonus images from some of our other fun dot-to-dot books

Find all of our books on Amazon

Beautiful Flowers and Butterflies
Dot-to-Dot for Adults

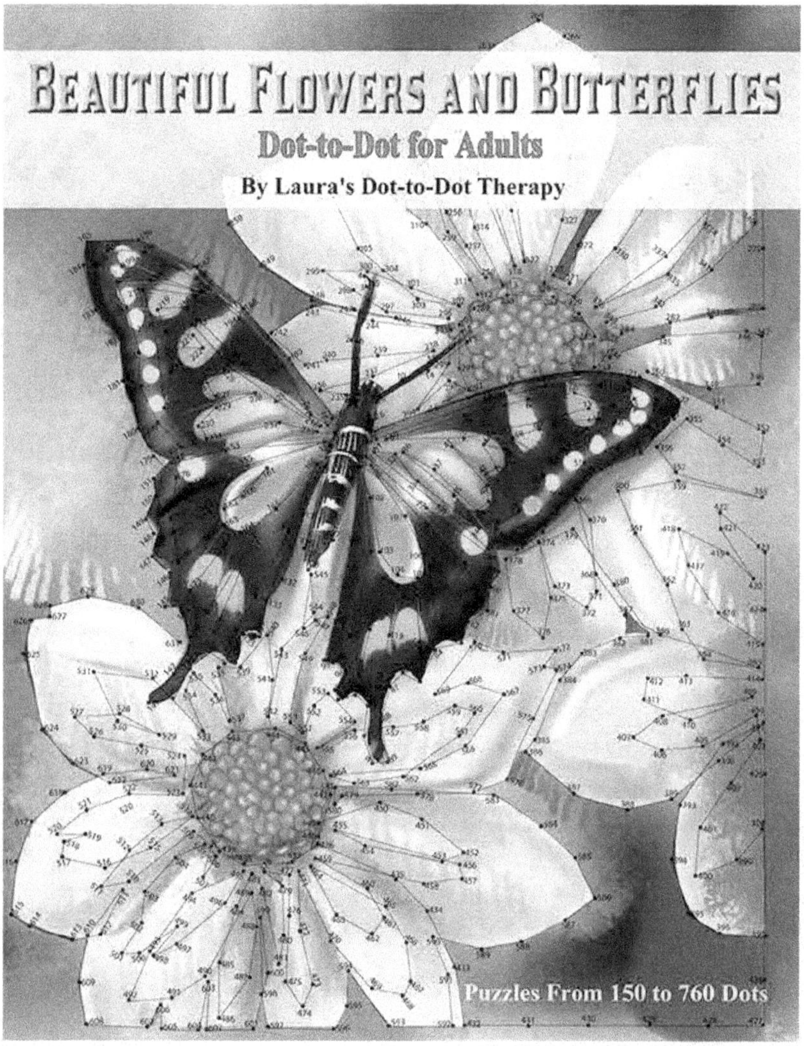

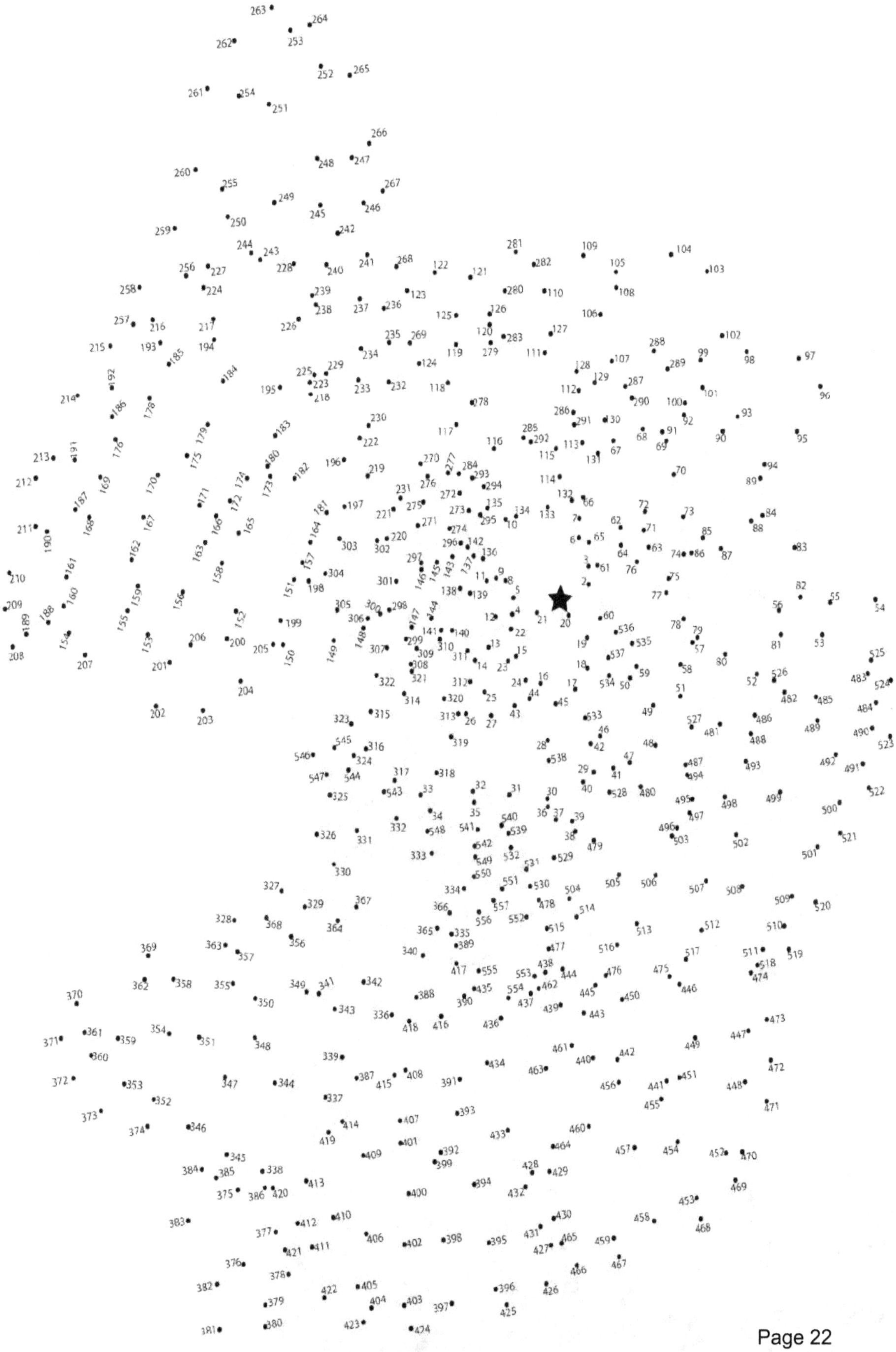

Mythical Mermaid
Dot-to-Dot Book for Adults
Puzzles from 150 to 750 Dots

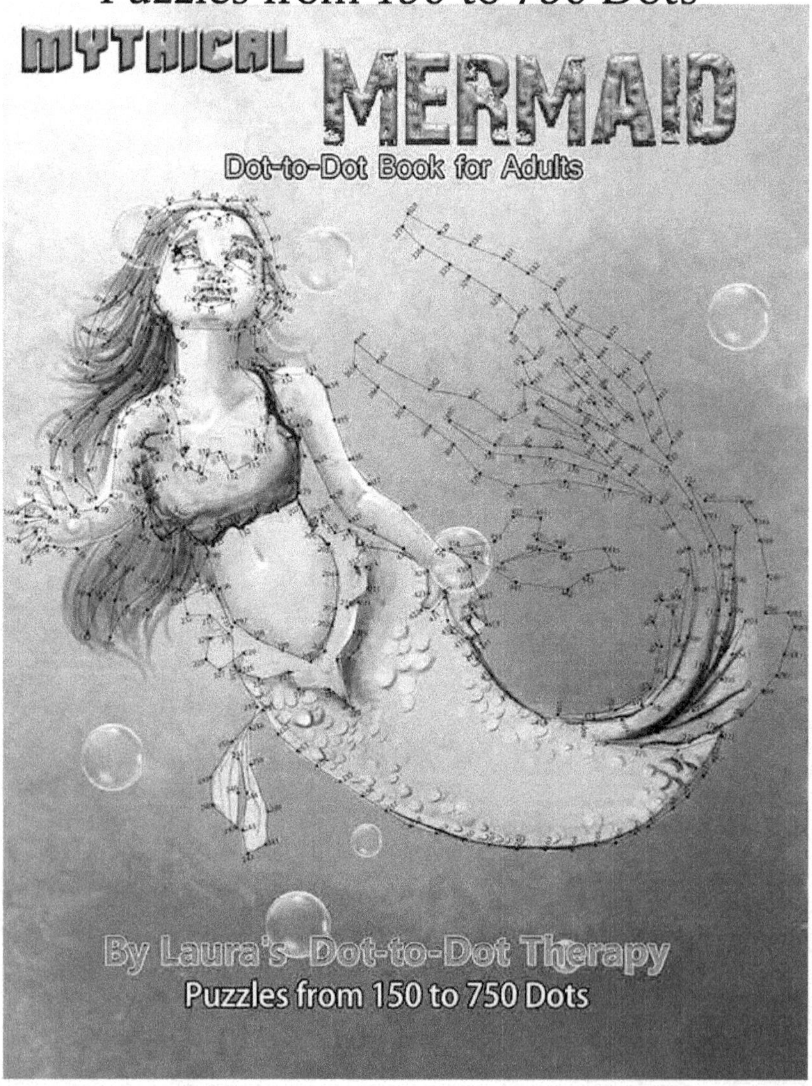

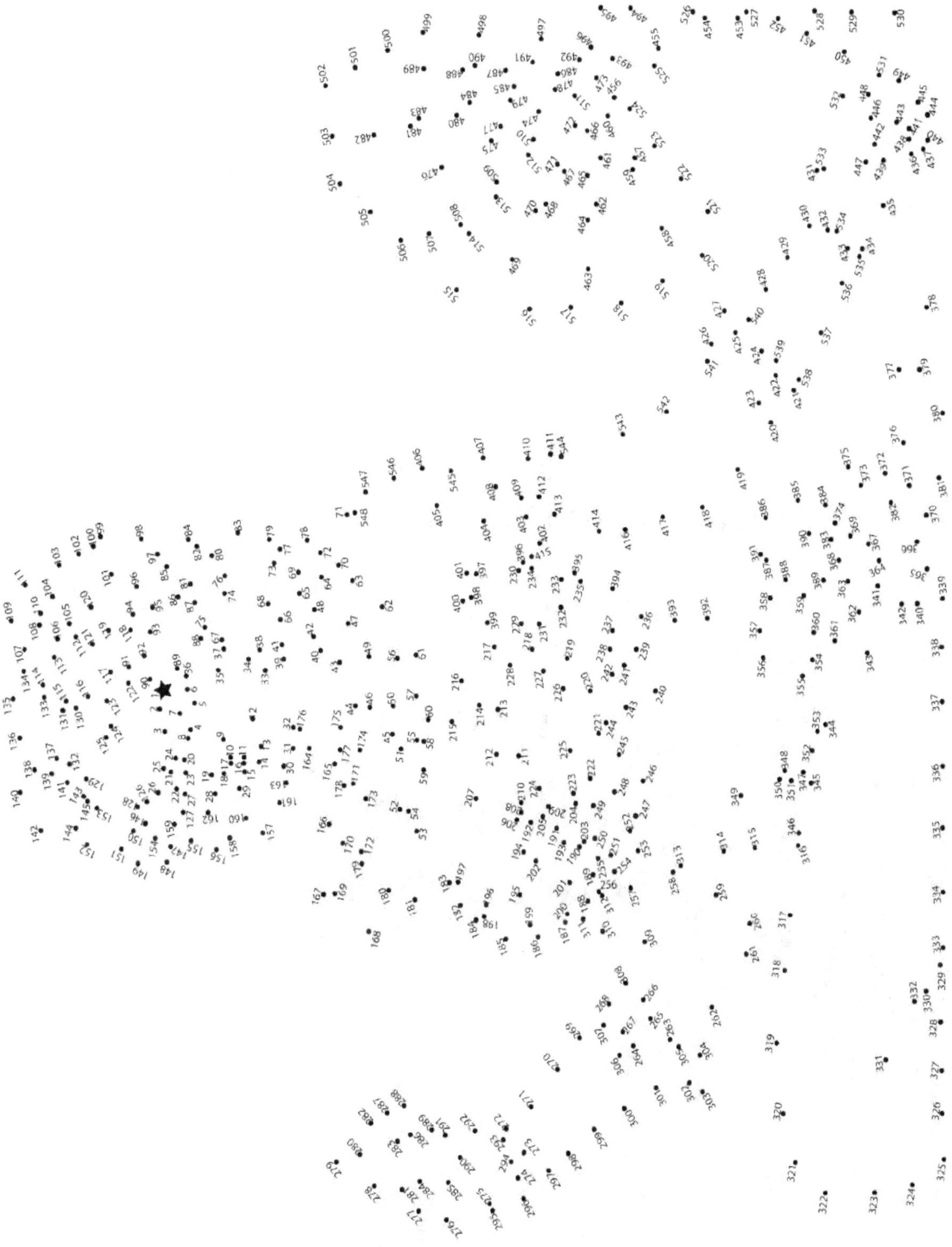

Famous Faces
Big Book of Extreme Dot to Dot

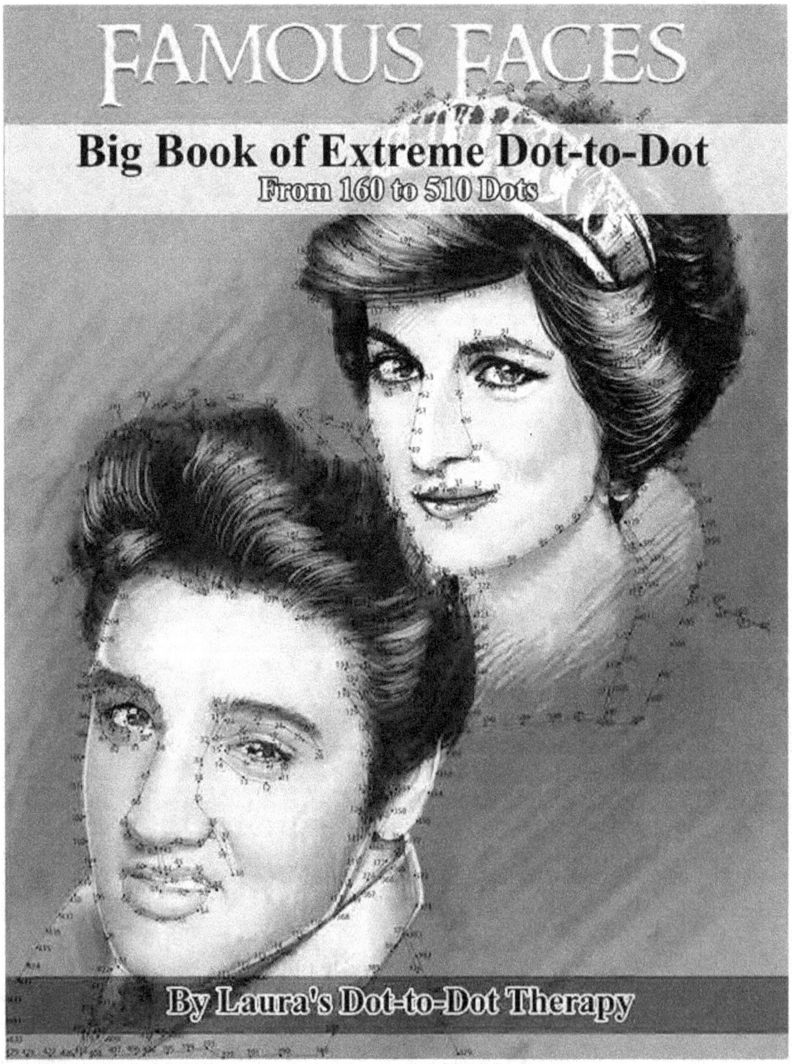

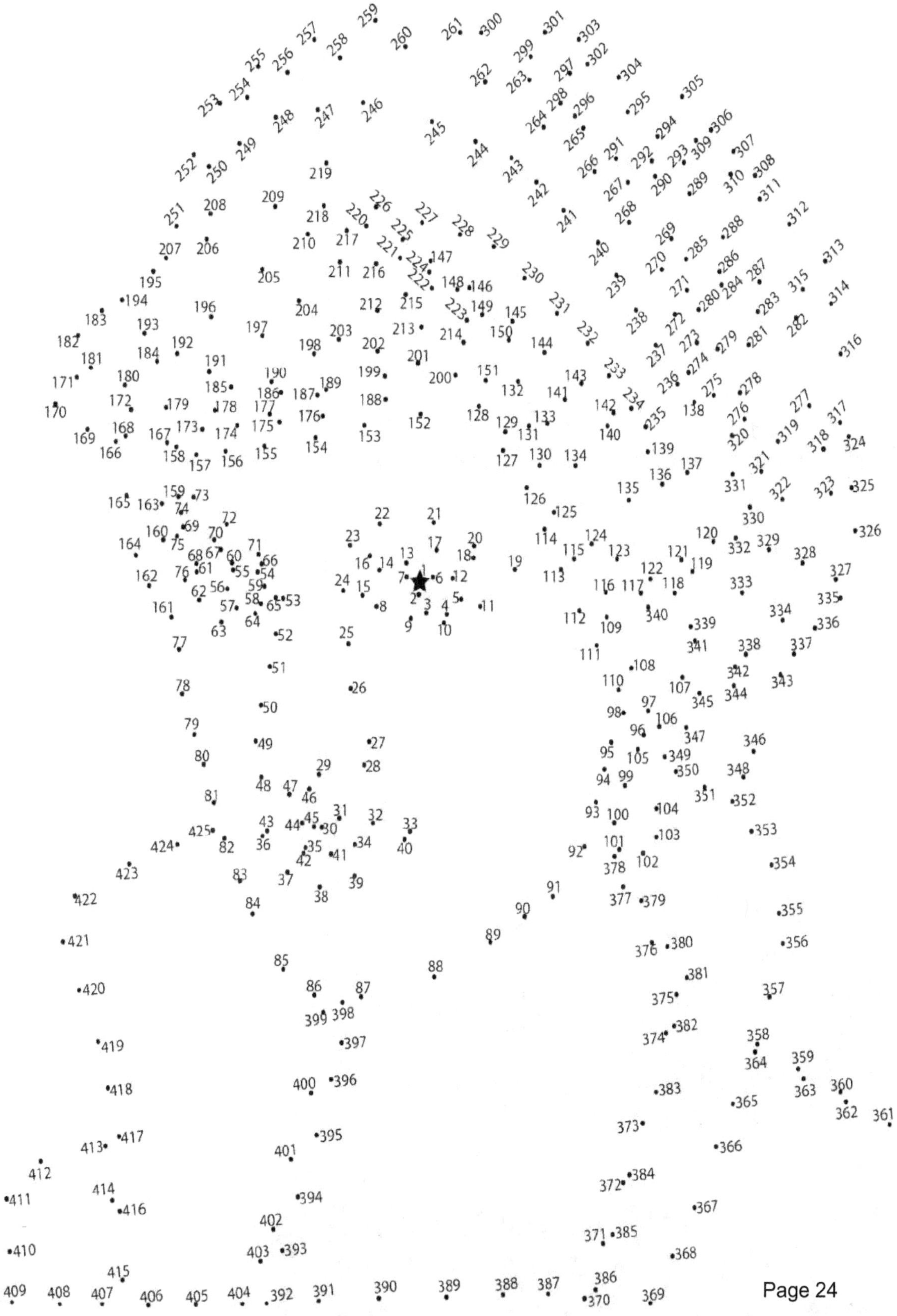

Antique Cars and Vintage Cars
Large Print Dot-to-Dot Book for Adults

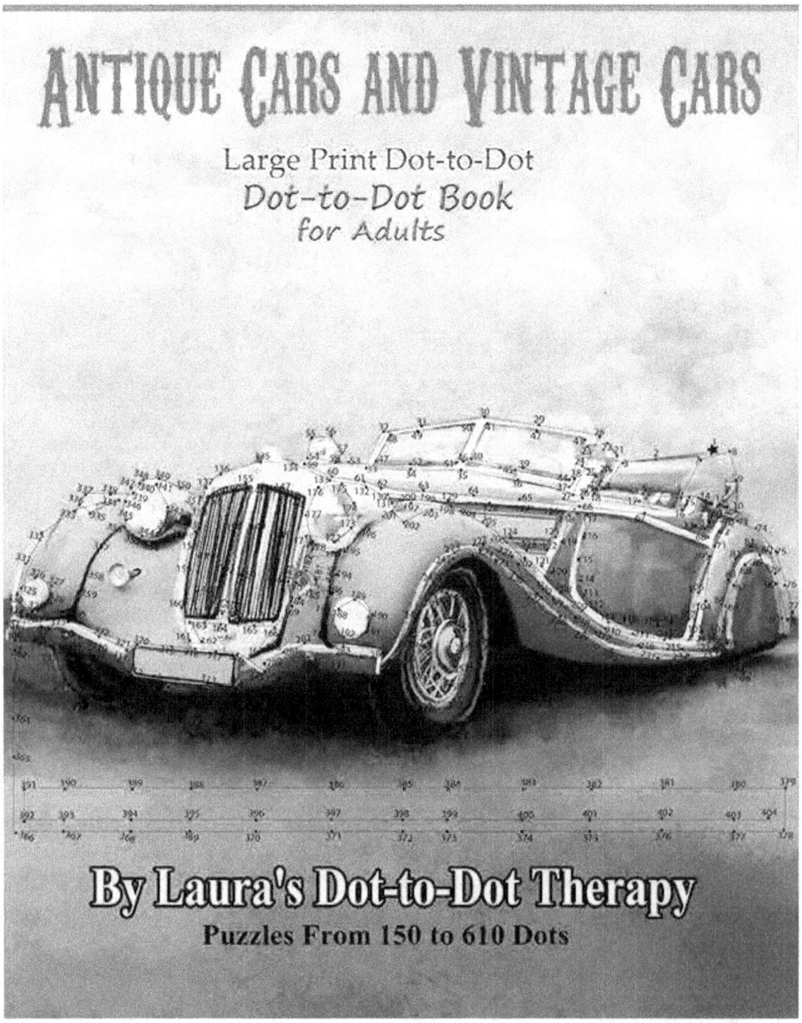

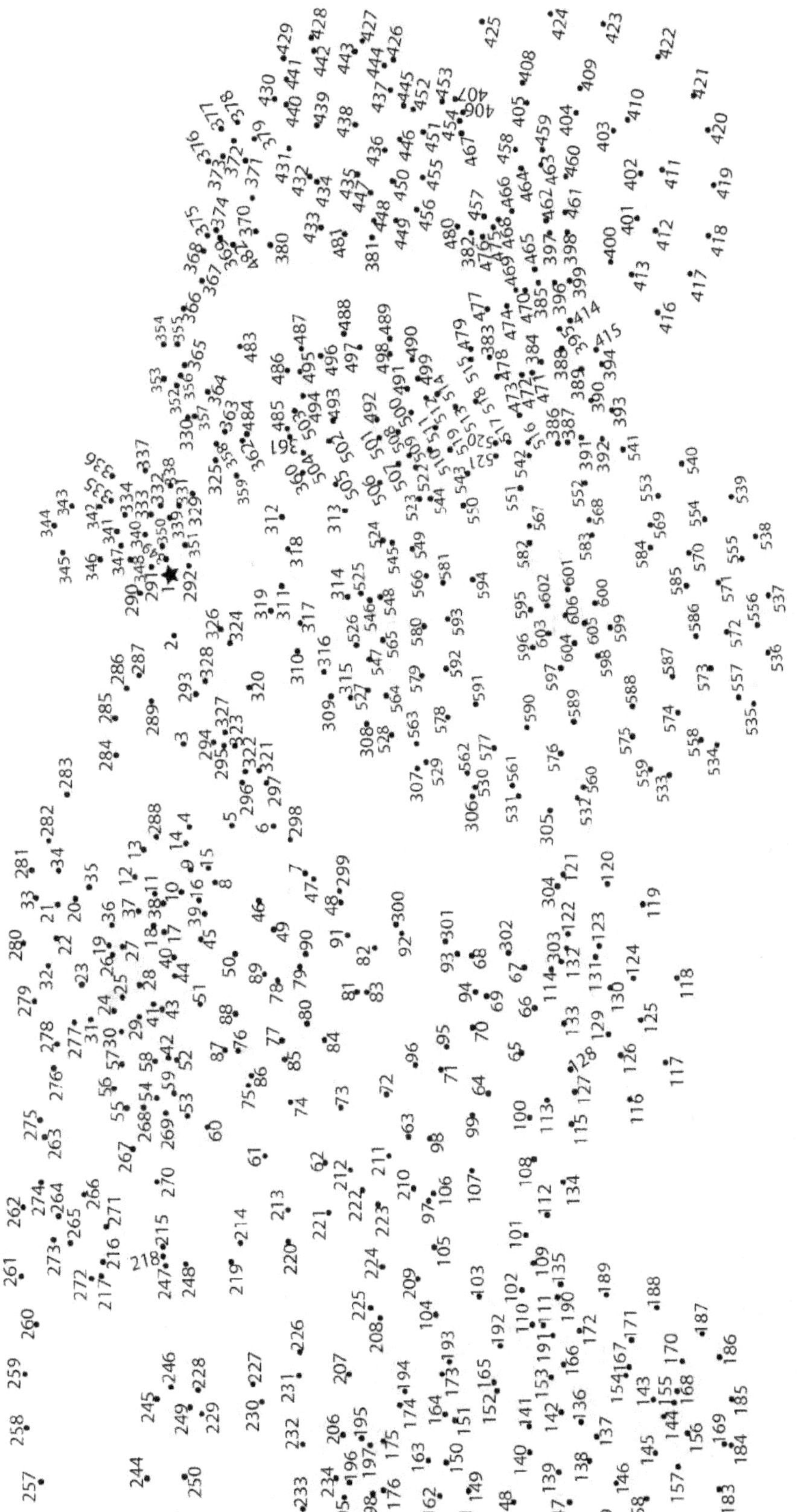

Easy to Read Large Print Dot to Dot
Beautiful Landscapes
Puzzles from 150 to 760 Dots

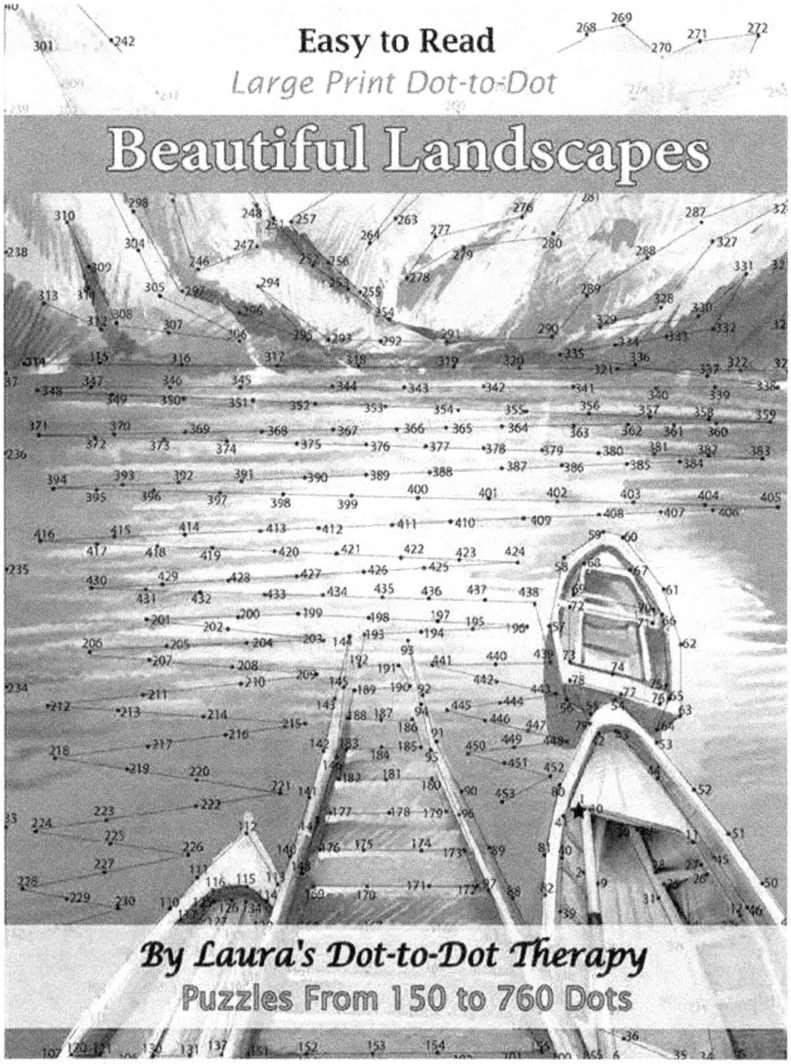

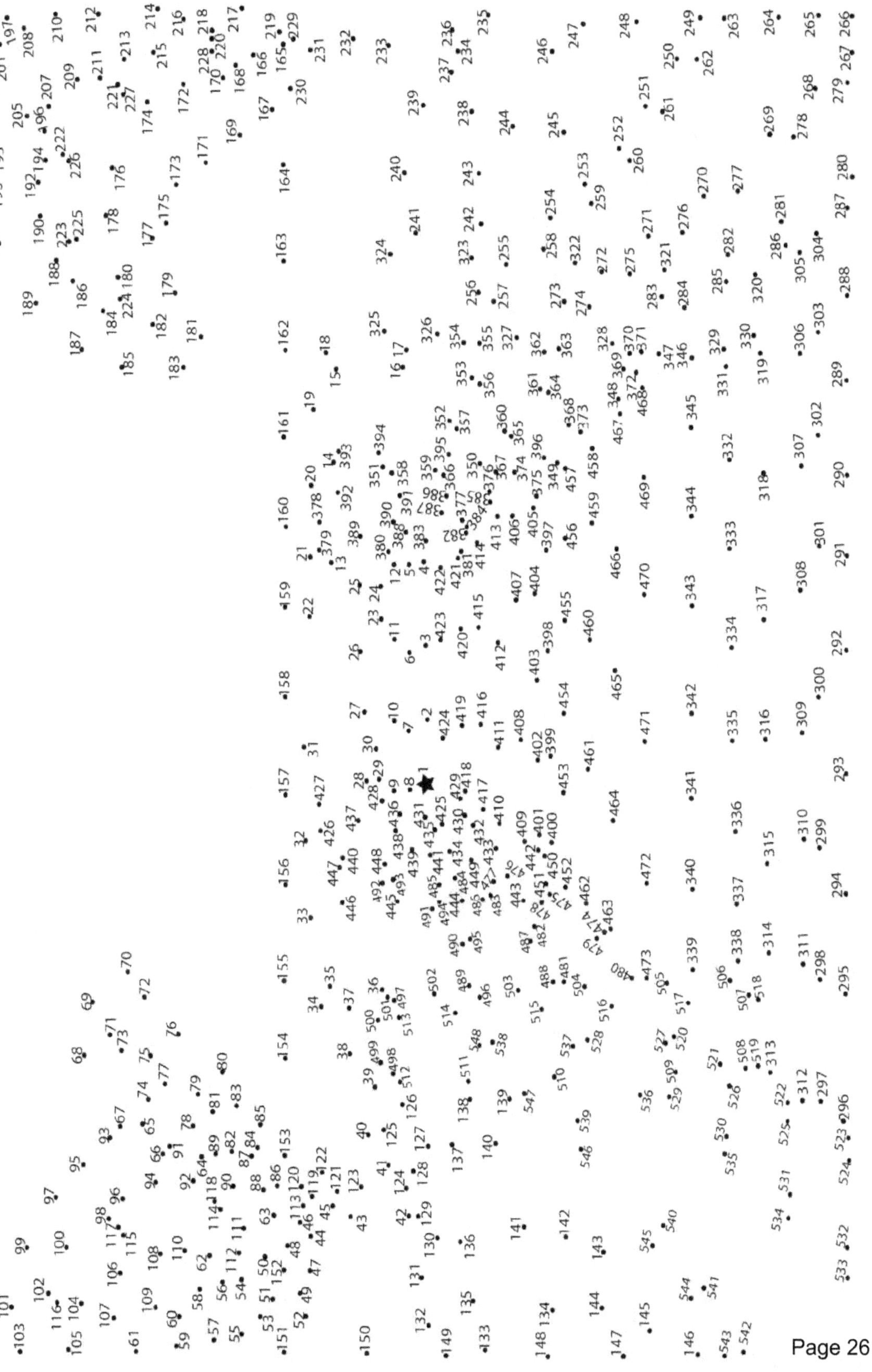

Answer Key

Follow along with the page numbers from top left to bottom right

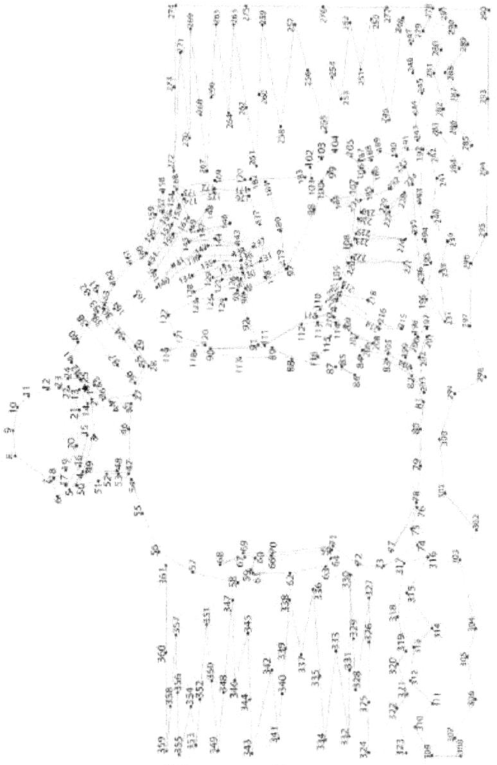

Page 1

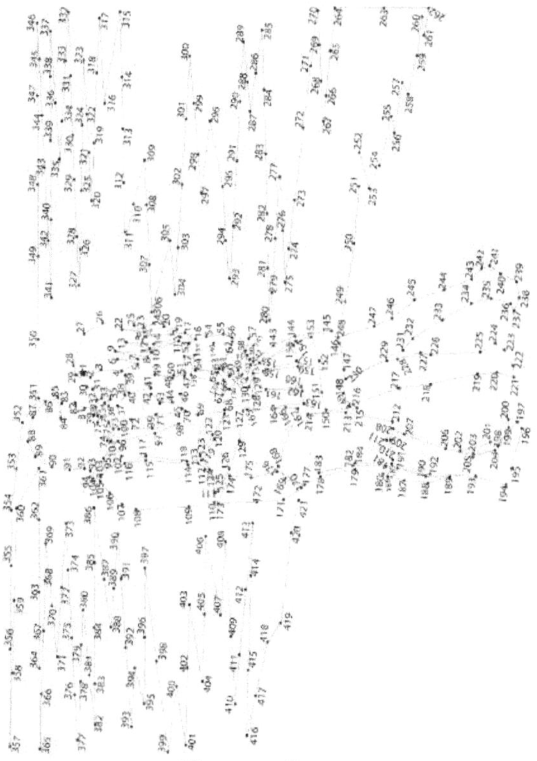

Page 2

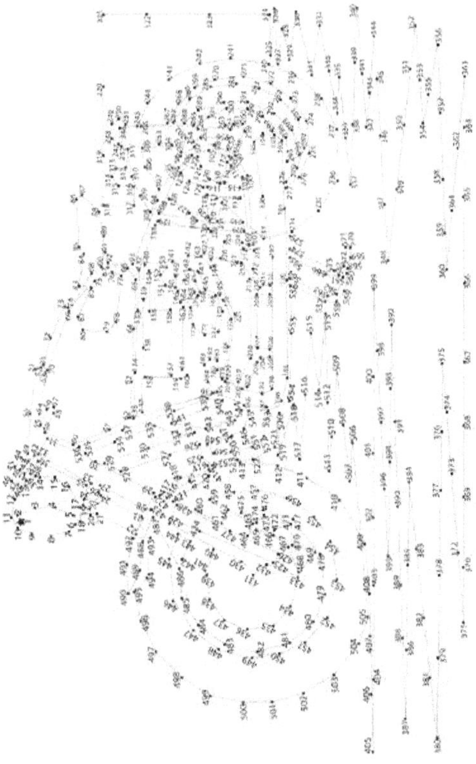

Page 3

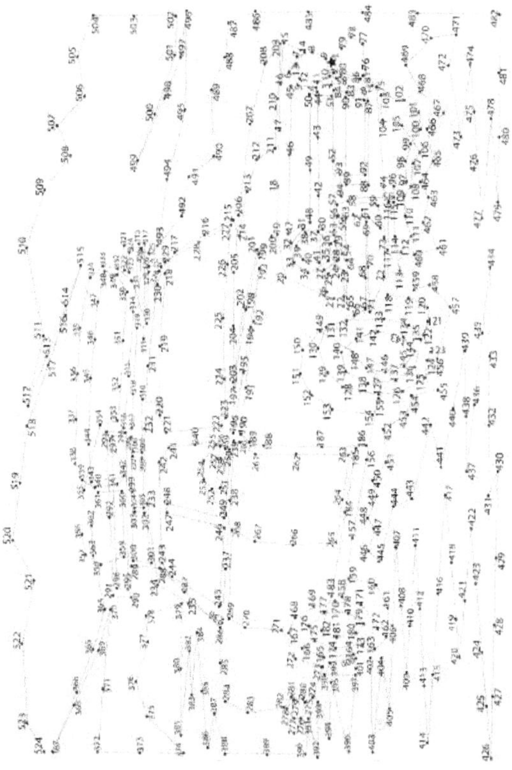

Page 4

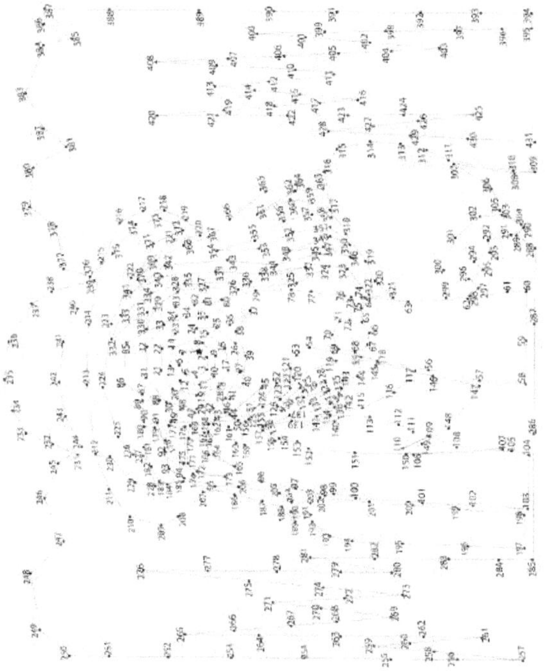

Page 5

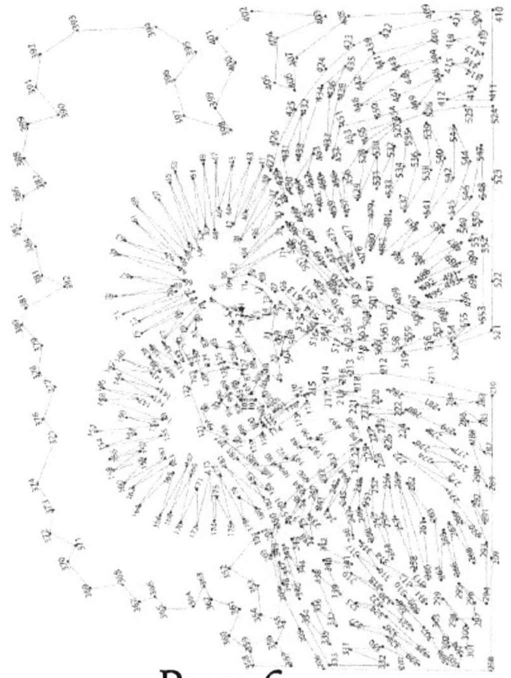

Page 6

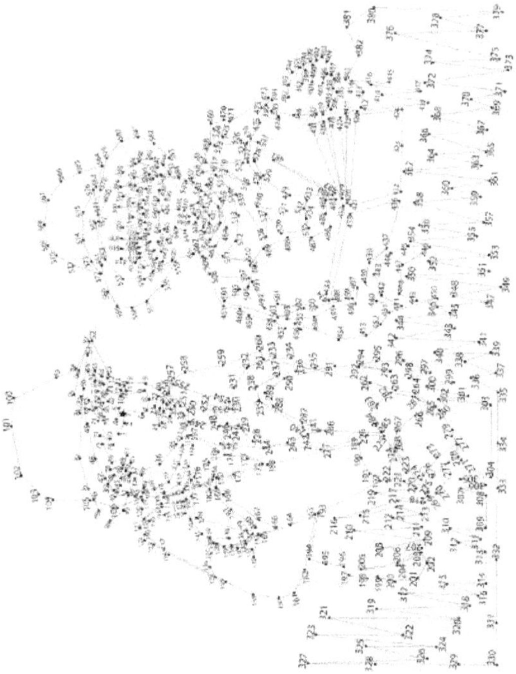

Page 7

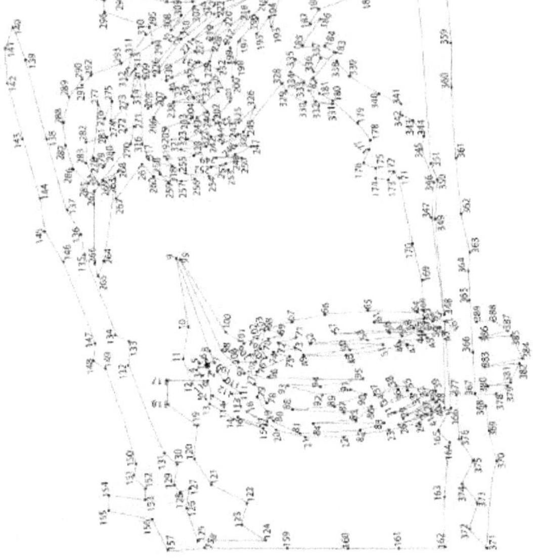

Page 8

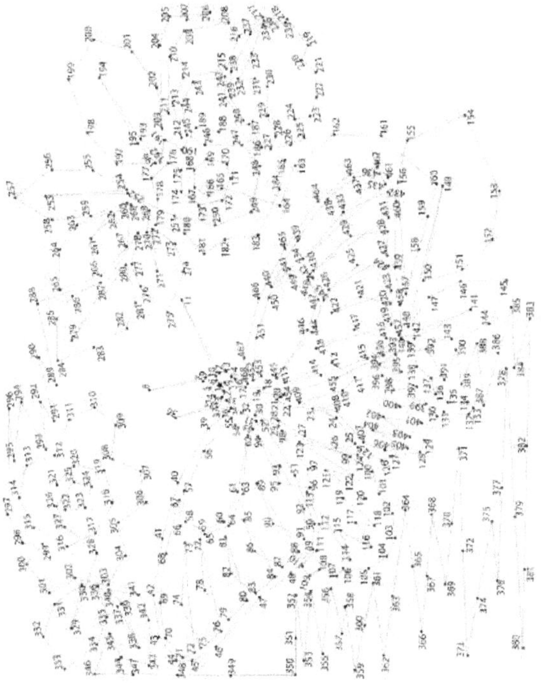

Page 9

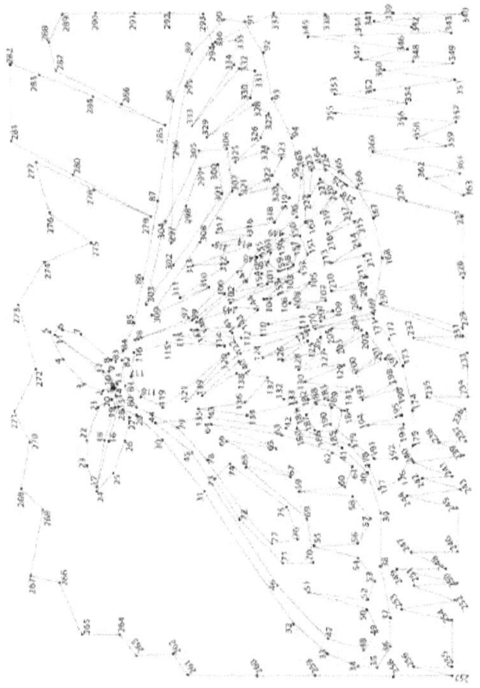

Page 10

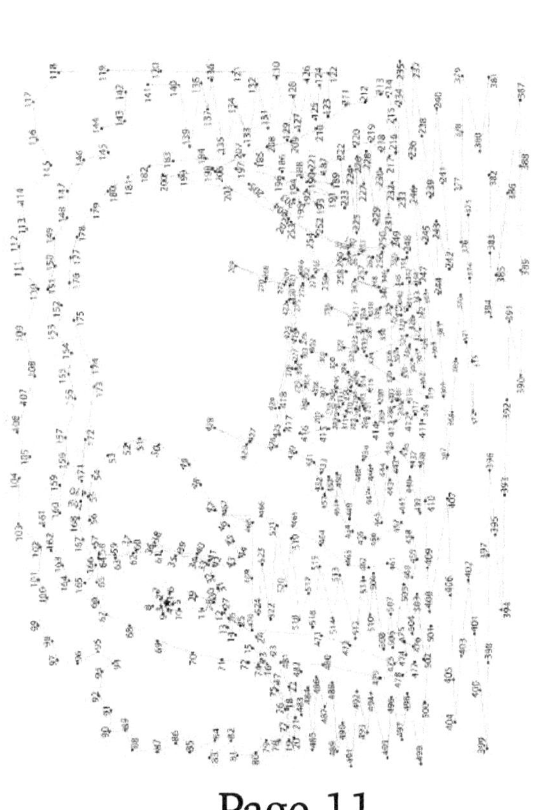

Page 11

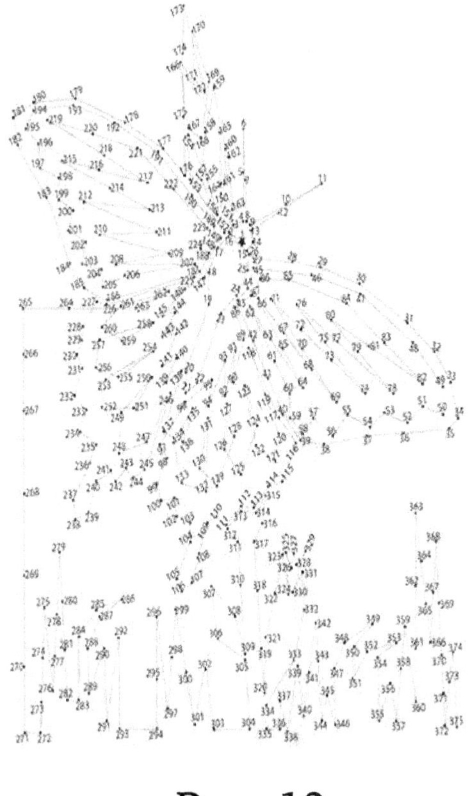

Page 12

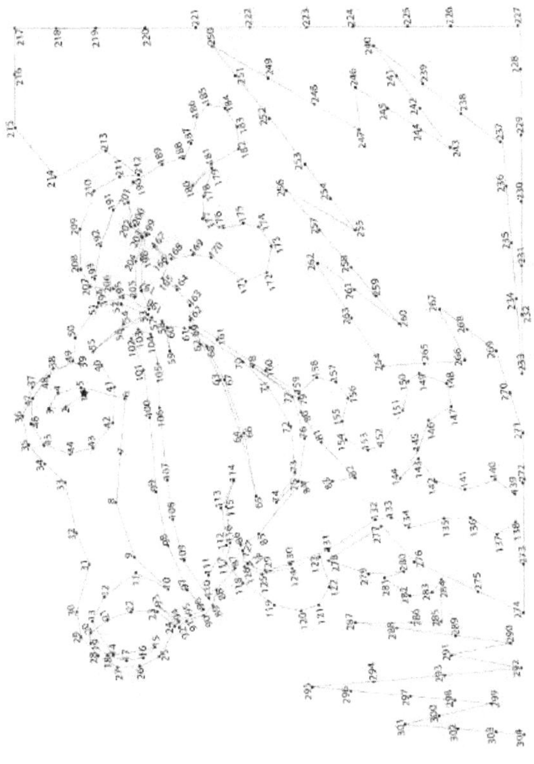

Page 13

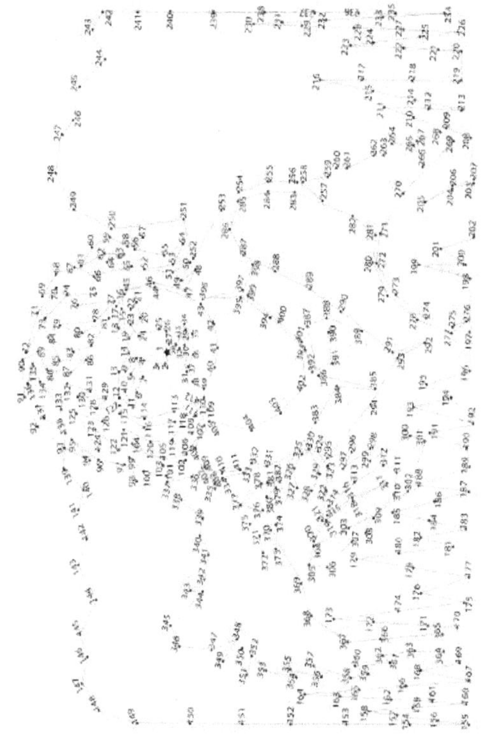

Page 14

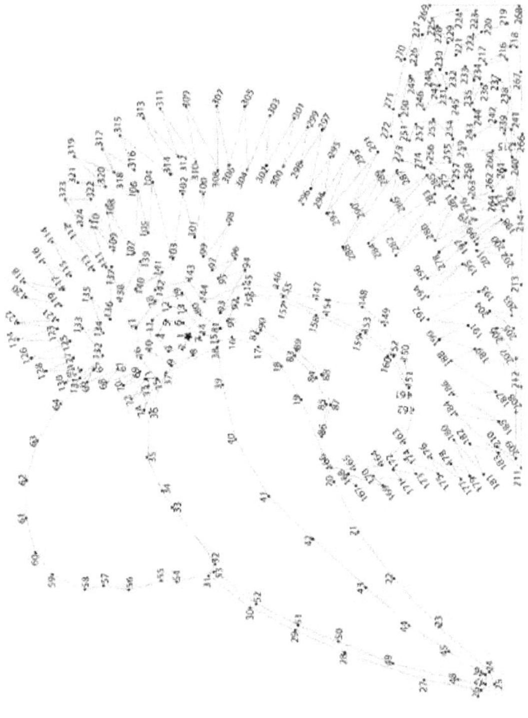

Page 15

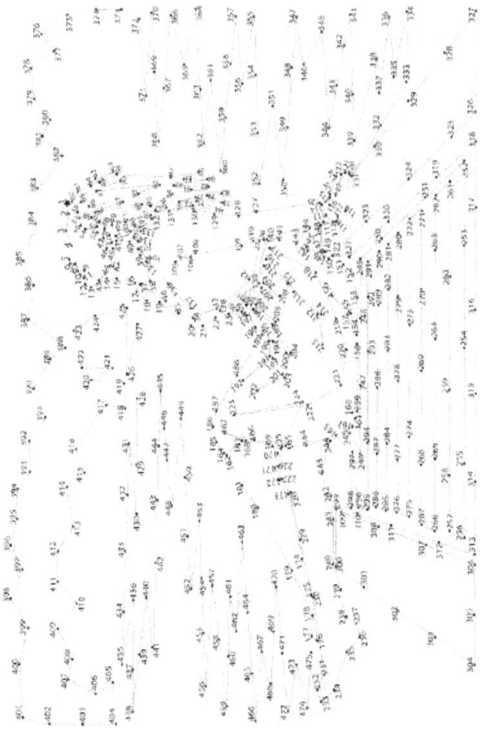

Page 16

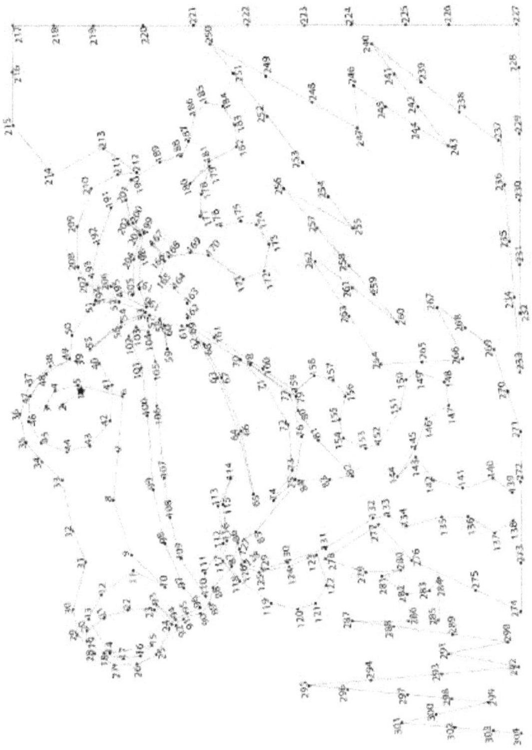
Page 13

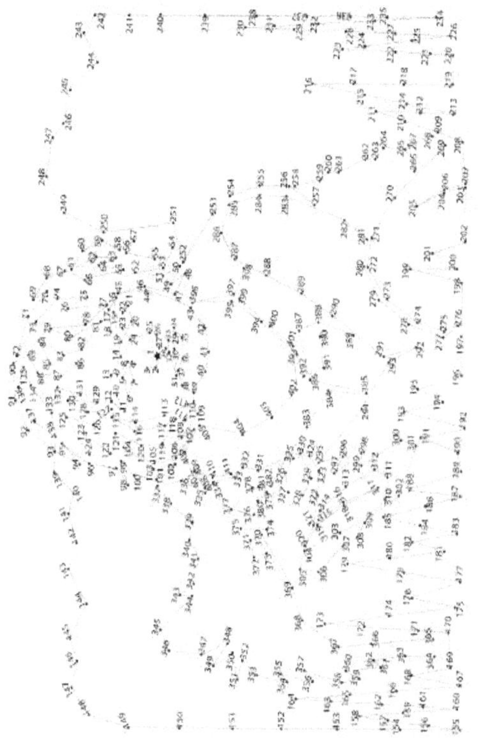
Page 14

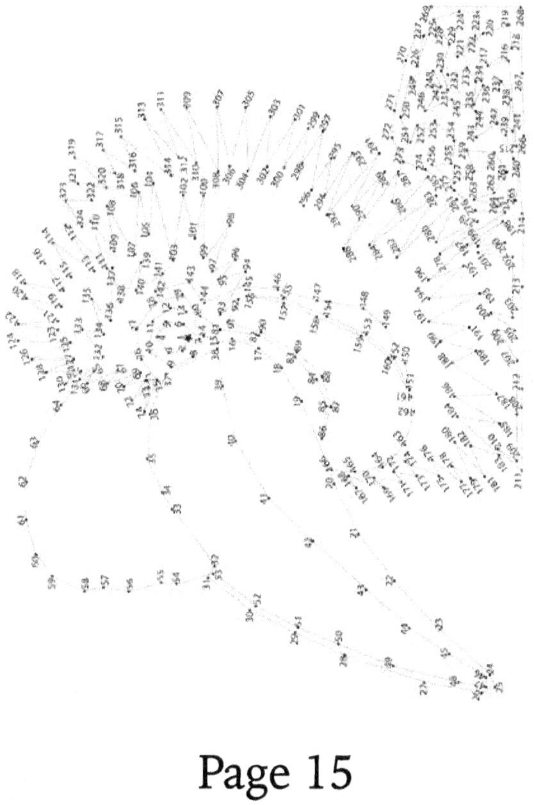
Page 15

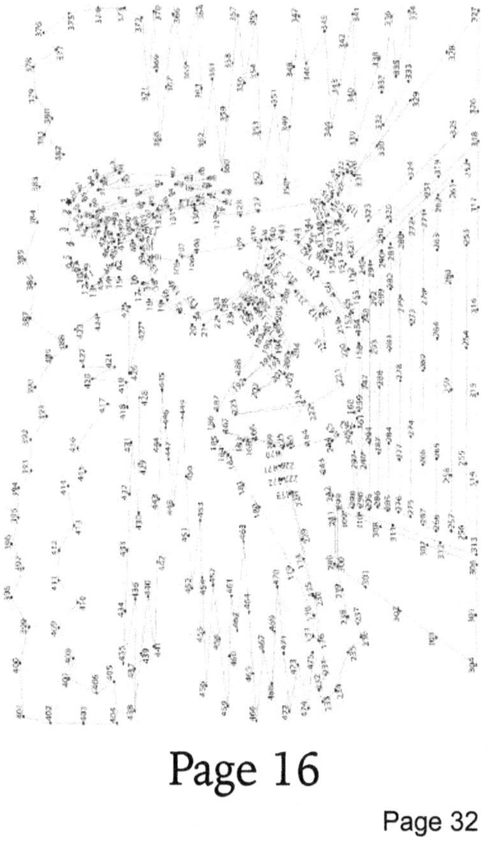
Page 16

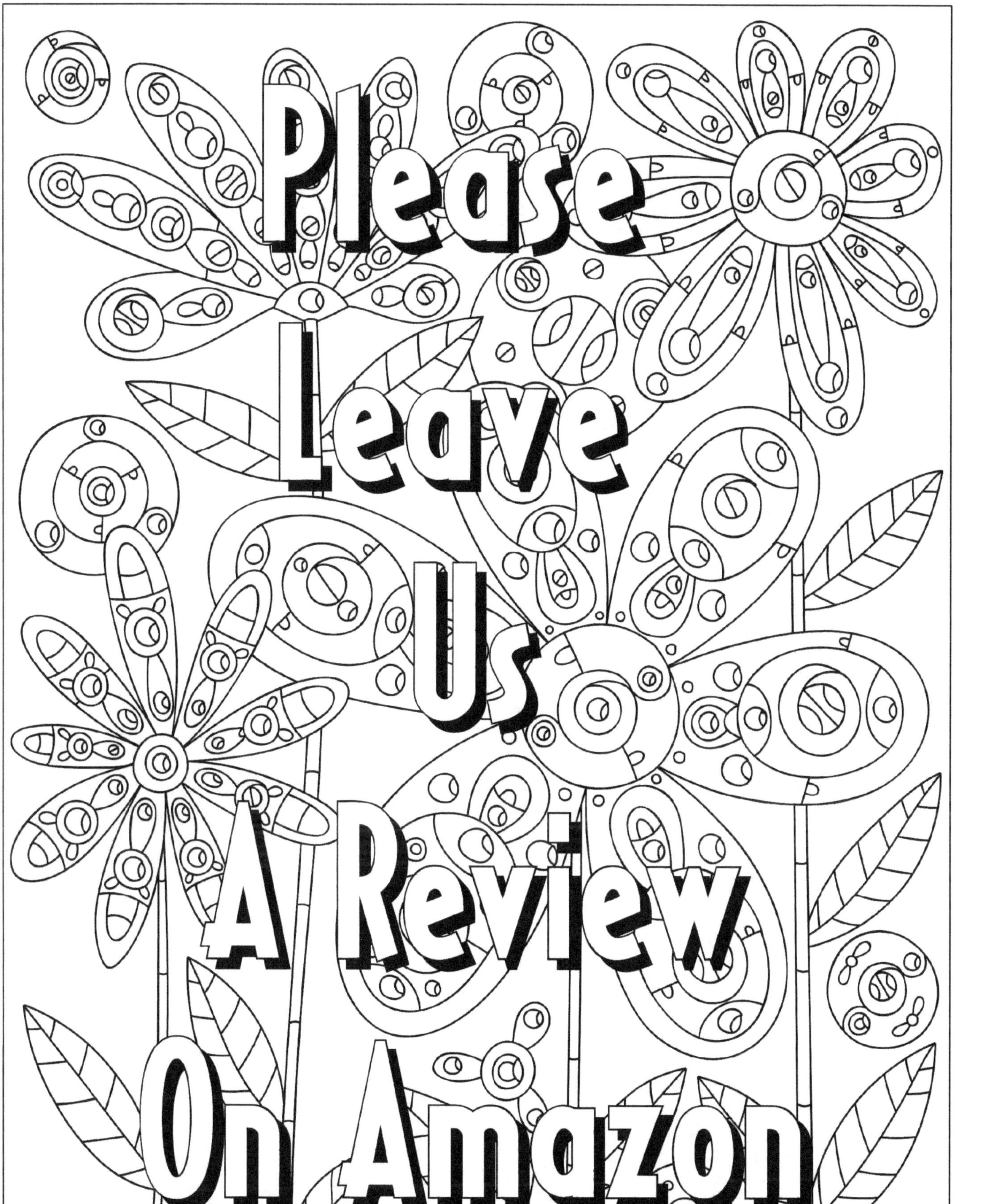
Please
Leave
Us
A Review
On Amazon

www.ingramcontent.com/pod-product-compliance
Lightning Source LLC
Chambersburg PA
CBHW081750220526
45468CB00008B/2323
* 9 7 8 1 7 9 2 1 0 6 5 6 9 *